Understanding
Yourself
and
Others™
Series

CHARACTER AND PERSONALITY TYPE

Discovering Your Uniqueness

FOR CAREER AND RELATIONSHIP SUCCESS

Dario Nardi

Telos
PUBLICATIONS
Huntington Beach, California

Understanding Yourself and Others and *The Temperament Matrix* are trademarks of Temperament Research Institute, Huntington Beach, California.

Myers-Briggs Type Indicator and *MBTI* are registered trademarks of Consulting Psychologists Press, Inc., Palo Alto, California.

Strong Interest Inventory is a registered trademark of Stanford University Press, Stanford, California.

PRINTED IN THE UNITED STATES OF AMERICA

Published By:

Telos Publications, a division of Temperament Research Institute
P.O. Box 4457, Huntington Beach, California 92605-4457
714.841.0041 or 800.700.4874 / fax 714.841.0312
www.telospublications.com / www.tri-network.com

International Standard Book Number: 0–9664624–6–7

04 03 02 01 00   10 9 8 7 6 5 4 3 2 1

Cover Photo: Norway Pine Bark
© 1998 Jim Brandenburg/Minden Pictures, used with permission.
Cover/Layout Design/Illustrations: Kristoffer R. Kiler
Character Illustrations: Joe Kohl
©1999 Temperament Research Institute, Exclusive World
Copyright, Used with Permission.
Illustrations: Chris Berens

ORDERING INFORMATION

Individual Sales U.S.: This publication can be purchased directly from Telos Publications at the address above.
Individual Sales International: Please contact Telos Publications at the address above for a list of international distributors.
Quantity Sales: Special discounts are available on quantity purchases by corporations, associations, and others. For details contact Telos Publications at the address above.
Orders for College Textbook/Course Adoption Use: Please contact Telos Publications at the address above.
Orders by U.S./International Trade Bookstores and Wholesalers: Please contact Telos Publications at the address above.

TRAINING AND CONSULTING INFORMATION

Individual Training: Training is available for further exploration of the information provided in this book. Please contact Temperament Research Institute at the address or telephone number above for a full curriculum schedule.
In-House Training and Consulting: Temperament Research Institute provides in-house training for communication, team building, leadership development, coaching, and organizational development.
Facilitator Training: Temperament Research Institute is an approved provider of Myers-Briggs Type Indicator® (MBTI®) Qualifying Programs. TRI also provides train-the-trainer workshops for temperament and the The Self-Discovery Process[SM].

This book is dedicated to my parents, all four of them.

A Special Thanks from Temperament Research Institute to those who made a unique contribution to make this book more friendly, helpful, and accurate.

Including Bonita Clark, Eric Conant, Laurie Duckworth, Linda Ernst, Mary Evans, Vicky Jo Varner, Melissa Smith, and Holly Wilson.

About the Author

Dario Nardi

Dario Nardi, Ph.D., is currently an adjunct assistant professor of mathematics at the University of California, Los Angeles, in the department's Program in Computing. He is the co-author of *The 16 Personality Types: Descriptions for Self-Discovery* and has authored several papers on type research with students. He has been working with type and temperament since 1992 and has been intimately involved in innovative product development with the Temperament Research Institute for seven years. Dario received his degree in systems science from the State University of New York at Binghamton's Watson School of Engineering. His background in systems thinking, linguistics and artificial intelligence, undergraduate curriculum design, and writing has led him to breakthroughs using multiple methods and models for getting at the "True Self," as well as for restructuring academic courses to suit all learning styles.

Contents

A Word from the Author

The inspiration for this book began with, and has been sustained by, the concerns voiced by many students and friends who have said they simply do not know what to do with their lives. With the success of similar books in the Understanding Yourself and Others series, I am now able to issue to the public and professionals character biographies of the various personality types.

At the heart of this work are the "biographies" - sixty-four brief character sketches based in part on interviews and experiences with real people, of each of the sixteen types. The biographies were not composed directly from theory. They are based on empirical observation - although a thorough knowledge of theory was vital to composing material that is balanced and consistent. They were put together in a holistic form that strives, in a brief sketch, to touch on many of the different aspects of personality and human experiences that influence who we are, what we do, how, and why.

While based on interviews, the character sketches are a product of one writer. Type biases; the influence of education, culture and gender in the writer's voice; and a number of other contextual factors present a challenge to you, the reader, to write your own personal sketch.

I am excited to say that in my experience, some people who have read these have discovered possible new directions and perspectives on their own type and personal development.

As an ongoing project, my goal is to generate dialogue in the type community about type clarification skills, the perceived "flavors" of each type, and the many issues around type development and character. Each sketch represents a different flavor, or aspect, of a type. I also see this as part of a larger recent movement toward thinking of the sixteen types as whole type patterns and in incorporating Jung's cognitive processes and the core needs, values, and talents described by Keirseyian temperament theory.

Thank you to Linda V. Berens and Kris Kiler at the Temperament Research Institute for their help in making this book possible; Stephanie Rogers for the first half-dozen short sketches she created - the seed for this project; my many students and friends who have contributed through feedback; and Sola Power for page 7 and her hours of help in exploring the many people who inhabit this world.

Dario Nardi
December 1999

Why?

Are you reading the want ads or handing out resumes, trying to improve your skills or looking for a job? Have you ever looked at the personal ads? In one or two lines a person has to sell themselves—to stand out from the crowd, to get the attention of someone he or she will hopefully be interested in. Or open up your school yearbook. What made you "you" to everyone else. Everyday we get up and see ourselves in the mirror and are called to examine our choices. What does it take to feel "I'm worth something?"

Self-Discovery

Who am I exactly? What are my unique talents, needs, values, and themes in life? How can I use these to further the development of who I am. Why am I on the planet?

Meeting Your Needs

If you are a manager, do your employees need more direction? How can you maximize their talents or help them escape an "us versus them" mind-set? Or perhaps you are a counselor or facilitator. How can you help each individual meet others at their view of the world? Or as a parent or teacher, is there a tool kit for your children and teens as they prepare to embark on their own life journey? And for yourself, are there keys to finding a successful balance between career and relationships?

Career Choice

What motivates me? I have several interests, how do I balance everything I want and need in a way that excites me and allows me to make something of myself?

How This Book Is Different

The self-discovery and self-leadership process outlined in this book is not about just making a one-time decision on a career or "fixing" a current relationship. This book is designed to give you the tools and some important organizing principles so that you can generate and maintain a life that offers sufficient choices, resources, and flexibility for you to respond to demands and opportunities over a lifetime.

Your Career and Relationships

Why do we get along with some people and not with others, whether in the office or in a relationship? And why do some careers and work environments excite and energize us and others turn us cold or terrify us? In all of life, some roads are open and some closed; some people we enjoy for the trip and others we tolerate. What is the best road?

Personal Relationships

Who am I compatible with? Congruence of values and beliefs is important. What about our personalities? Why am I even in a relationship with this person?

How to Use This Book

Before we begin a journey we need to know what to pack and what might be left to pick up along the way. And we need a compass, a map, and the tools to draw a new map when we reach uncharted territory. Your compass for discovery here is the theory of temperament. Your tools are the eight life-themes, and your map of possibilities is the sixty-four biographies and the many ways people are similar and different.

People Skills

How can I better understand and get along with the people around me, my parents, siblings, friends, boss, and colleagues? What's necessary to know before helping others?

Discovering Your Uniqueness

The Roots of Character

Character has many meanings, and a broad philosophical perspective of character asks us to believe that we all make decisions and try to develop in the best way we can, given our inherent nature, life background, current resources and future potential. Sometimes this process seems difficult and possibly painful. More often, given a push in the right direction, small day-to-day decisions about how we lead our lives amplify into lasting effects. In this sense, character becomes a particular pattern of characteristic choices and changes as opposed to a simple linear scale or static set of either/or options.

Character as Personality Pattern

Different personality theories—temperament, type, cognitive processes, interaction styles—describe different aspects of our inborn preferences and tendencies. Each of us has access in some way to the entire range of the human experience. However, when we know what we prefer—the needs, values, themes and talents that best describe our inborn self—we are freer to be ourselves and freer to welcome others from their perspectives. We move from futile attempts to change others to a productive life of working with people.

Character as Life-Themes

Character can refer to fiction. We create stories for ourselves and the people around us about who we are and who they are—and were, should be, can be, and will be. Stories provide meaningful answers to the basic human questions: Why do I exist? What is my purpose? What do I believe and not believe? Rigid stories are draining and limiting. We "have no choice." Rich stories allow us to answer the human questions in a way that is not static but dynamic, creative, and life-giving. And there is something to learn from each story.

Character as Morals and Ethics

Character in a moral sense is a distinctive mark about the choices and changes we have made over the course of our lives under a variety of seemingly difficult, unfair, and uncertain conditions. We and our ethical covenants are imperfect. We make compromises. In particular, character is about how we deal with the call to keep growing and how to deal with the consequences—

intended or not—that result from our thoughts, words, actions and creative contributions. What and who are we responsible for each day and to what extent?

While each person is unique, we can talk about the common ingredients that contribute to our sense of uniqueness.

Character is not an isolatable compartment in the brain, a single story or a rigid set of ethical standards. Rather, a broad definition includes the narrow definitions, each aspect of character explaining and enriching the others. Circumstances may hide strong character, but there is only one of you in all of history. Character results from what the world gives us and how we choose to act and respond. It is an on-going process we are called to actively cultivate. It reflects everything that we do and everything that we are. Character emerges from our true self.

Understanding Yourself*

Just as there are multiple meanings of character, so too are there several ways to view one's "self." It is as if we have different "selves."

The Contextual Self

The *contextual self* is who we are in any given environment. It is how we behave depending on what the situation requires. Here is where our flexibility and adaptability come into play. We have many tools and resources to help us adapt to the needs of a situation. These tools may be concrete resources, types of intelligences, motivating beliefs, special gifts or talents we possess, or even the fruits of our needs and values. The more skill and comfort we have with any one tool, the more likely we are to use that one in a certain context. However, a specific environment may require, push us to use, or even give us a skill in new areas.

The Developed Self

When the *contextual self* becomes habitual and ongoing, it becomes a part of the *developed self.* Several factors influence development. First, inborn tendencies have a natural way of unfolding and developing. Given our tendencies, we are more likely to develop some aspects of our personalities at different times in life and even avoid or ignore others.

* Adapted, with permission, from Linda V. Berens, Dario Nardi, *The 16 Personality Types: Descriptions for Self-Discovery* (Huntington Beach, CA.: Telos Publications, 1999)

The responses of the environment as we engage with it can also subtly influence our development. If we are rewarded for certain behaviors and punished for others, we can't help but be influenced.

But we also make choices and changes as we exercise our free will in response to what life presents us. We internalize our beliefs. Others also influence our roles and interactions.

The True Self

An aspect of our personality and character exists from the beginning of our lives. This aspect of ourselves is in our genes, our DNA. We are born with a tendency to behave in certain ways, which influences how we adapt, grow and develop and what we value. When we act in congruence with this true self, we are more likely to be in a state of "flow," or high energy. When we have to act in ways that are different, we are likely to pay a high energy cost. So we may pay a price when a situation and our development requires tools and gifts that are different from our natural inclinations and core values.

In understanding ourselves, it is important to understand all of these "selves" and to honor the ways we can be in all instances. It is important to not limit our self-knowledge to just our *contextual self*, our *developed self* or our *true self*.

**One powerful way to find your *true self*
is through self-discovery.**

A Process of Self-Discovery

When we seek to understand our "self," we may find each of our "selves" quite similar or quite different from the others. For example, we might naturally prefer different tools than are required by the current context. This is one reason why trying to figure out the true self is difficult when we look at a single behavior or value. Another reason is that we may have adapted to life's challenges by suppressing some of our natural inclinations and by developing abilities that are not part of our natural pattern. When these processes have become an integral part of our developed self, it is often very difficult to determine our true self. No one personality instrument, career or values inventory, or single view of character or personality will by itself easily get at the true self. A variety of approaches works best in exploring the "self."

Self-Reflection

We have found that identification of one's true self is not easy to do when trying to decide between, say, either/or dichotomous preferences. This is because day-to-day life requires us to use more than our preferences, and certain tasks, roles, and environments draw on different talents and resources. You will have several opportunities to reflect on how your unique character can emerge and express itself in your career and relationships.

Interaction with Others— Sharing and Feedback

We also learn who we are through our interactions with others. Finding people who are similar to us and comparing notes and sharing stories helps many of us discover our true self. One valuable way of finding out who we are is by actively seeking feedback–asking others to tell us how they see us. These people may be trained facilitators or merely people who know us well. And remember this feedback is a gift, often given through the eyes of the giver, so seek feedback from many people.

Openness to New Information

Many variables are involved in self-discovery, and during the process "unconscious" information sometimes comes into our minds–aspects previously unknown to ourselves or to others. The unconscious is often where we "store" information about how to "be" in the world. Be aware that family, social, cultural and other influences will affect how you view yourself and what kinds of decisions you initially feel comfortable with. These influences are often unconscious until they are described and pointed out. Rejecting what clearly doesn't fit is also an important part of the process as long as you remain open and searching. As you explore who you are, stay open to valuable insights from many sources.

Five Easy Steps

1. Discover your best-fit temperament and personality type as a compass for your journey.
2. Explore eight common life-themes and find which career and relationship stories balance your needs and values.
3. Read and analyze holistic biographical character sketches to find your own uniqueness.
4. Explore the relationship and career decisions you've made in life that explain your personal "flavor," including important ethical choices, common pitfalls, and contributions.
5. Integrate your understandings and explorations as part of rewriting your future.

Using Your Experiences

We are in the world, and character is how we act and respond to the situations and relationships that the world presents to us.

Take a few minutes to reflect and identify some of your experiences and sources of stress in past or current situations.

Think of the best job or relationship you've ever had (or perhaps a school or group experience). What made it the best? What needs and values were met or talents used? What parts came naturally and easily?

Best Relationship or Career Experience

Worst Relationship or Career Experience

Now, think of the worst job or relationship you've ever had. What made it the worst? What needs and values were violated or talents unused? What drained your energy?

What comes to mind when you think of someone who has character?

Life experiences demonstrate to us that people are very different in their needs, values and talents. Even those who share some aspects in common can differ significantly in other ways. For centuries people have been trying to categorize these patterns into personality styles. Among these ways is the theory of temperament.

Temperament*—Your Compass for Discovery

What Is Temperament?

Temperament is a framework for understanding personality. Temperament is also interpersonal: it describes patterns of interaction that arise between people with different core needs and values. The origins of temperament theory go back twenty-five centuries! Philosophers through the ages have identified four basic kinds of people in the world. And we can identify which of the four categories a person ultimately belongs to by observing their actions and natural talents, listening to their language and what they choose to discuss, understanding what values they hold dear, and knowing what is the fundamental motivating force in their lives.

Four Types of Intelligence

One way to look at the four temperaments is as four intelligences–how we organize, interact with, move through, and give meaning to our environment and the people in it.

DIPLOMATIC INTELLIGENCE

To build bridges between people, to have empathy, to strive to unify by understanding and resolving deeper issues while honoring individual uniqueness, to move to a level of abstraction to see how two seemingly different views are alike and then to choose a symbolic way of communicating the similarity.

LOGISTICAL INTELLIGENCE

To get the right things and the right information, in the right place, at the right time, in the right quantity, in the right quality, to the right people and not to the wrong people. To attend to people's comforts, to make it easy for others. To make sure everything is taken care of so things go right and things don't go wrong.

STRATEGIC INTELLIGENCE

To think of and explain all the possible contingencies and influencing factors and then design processes for achieving the objectives, to abstractly analyze a situation and consider previously unthought-of possibilities, to look at the relationships between the goals and the means.

TACTICAL INTELLIGENCE

To read the current context, the situation, and skillfully manage the situation to effect a desired result, often coming up with a variety of solutions; to take action according to the needs of the moment and plan the next move; to cleverly display, compose and perform with attention to impact and effect.

Now think back to the best job or class that you've had and your worst job or class. What skills, talents, interests–what intelligence–did that allow you, or not allow you, to use?

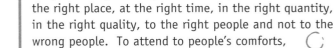

▼ C H A R A C T E R ▼

Character as a personality pattern: Temperament characterizes our core needs, values, and talents and reveals where others come from as well as a personal path for success.

* The brief temperament overview on pages 5, 6 and 8 is taken in part from Linda V. Berens, *Understanding Yourself and Others: An Introduction to Temperament*, (Telos Publications, Huntington Beach, CA.: 1998).

Core Needs and Values

Another aspect of temperament is core needs and values. Read and rate each of the four categories below. Rate them as a whole. That is, pay less attention to the meaning of individual words, and more attention to the overall theme that the words imply, taken together. (For example, responsibility can have many meanings, but taken together with words like *tradition* and *safety* and *structure*, a particular kind of "managerial" or "protective" responsibility is implied.)

Idealist, Rational, Guardian and Artisan name the four basic patterns of personalities.

IDEALIST	GUARDIAN
Significance	Tradition
Authenticity	Responsibility
Unique Identity	Group Membership
Personal Meaning	Safety and Security
Ethics	Structure
Diplomacy	Logistics

RATIONAL	ARTISAN
Knowledge	Adapting to the Moment
Competence	Freedom to Act
Self Mastery	Making an Impact
Progress	Variety
Concepts	Motive
Strategy	Tactics

> Now look back at the best relationship or social experience that you've had and your worst relationship or social experience. What made it best or worst? What core needs and values did that relationship or social experience support or not support?

Meeting Your Core Needs and Values in Career and Relationships

Like a tree trunk, each temperament has a core from which all growth and rejuvenation originates. The growing part of a tree is at the center and growth emanates outward from that center. If that center is damaged or diseased, the tree dies. For a temperament pattern, the growing part is the core needs and values. It is only when these core needs are met that the individual is energized and truly high functioning. To not have the core needs

met is like "psychological death" and is one source of stress or even dysfunctional behavior. Similarly, pursuing the core needs and values gives the individual the greatest sustenance. In contrast, around the core is the inner bark of a tree, which provides the transport of food to growing sections. These outer parts of the tree are like talents or favorite abilities and roles. By exercising these talents and playing temperament-specific roles, we bring new energy to ourselves. These talents and roles are well suited to meet one's temperament needs.

Temperament and Stress

For each temperament, there are key stressors, different expressions of stress, and 'antidotes' for that stress. Whether at school, at work or at home, stress is what happens when our temperament needs and values are not being met and our talents are not being utilized. Stress behavior happens in a pattern. For example, an Idealist might experience insincerity, abandonment or boredom, but only insincerity would lead to phoniness.

IDEALIST	GUARDIAN
STRESSORS	**STRESSORS**
Insincerity	Abandonment
Betrayal	Insubordination
Lack of Integrity	Lack of Belonging
WHEN STRESSED	**WHEN STRESSED**
Dissociates	Complains
Becomes Phony	Becomes "Sick, Tired, Sorry, Worried"
ANTIDOTES FOR STRESS	**ANTIDOTES FOR STRESS**
Affirmation & Nurturing from Self & Others	Inclusion in News & Activities, Appreciation
New 'Quests'	New Membership

RATIONAL	ARTISAN
STRESSORS	**STRESSORS**
Powerlessness	Constraint
Incompetence	Boredom
Lack of Knowledge	Lack of Impact
WHEN STRESSED	**WHEN STRESSED**
Obsesses	Retaliates
Becomes Mindless	Becomes Reckless
ANTIDOTES FOR STRESS	**ANTIDOTES FOR STRESS**
Reconfirmation of Competence & Knowledge	Find Options & New Ways to Have Impact
A New Project	New Activities

How we experience stress is just one of many ways that temperament patterns our lives.

What Makes You Unique?

Each of the four temperaments views uniqueness through a different lens. Here are some examples.

Typical Idealist Responses

For many Idealists, uniqueness can be thought of as our inherent nature or gifts in life. It's something unique about each person, like the sister who can draw how people feel or the person who can play music that moves others or the boyfriend who has a heart. What each of them is doing isn't so unique, but for each of them the way they do what they do feels unique while they are doing it. More than the other temperaments, Idealists ponder what characterizes uniqueness, both for themselves and others, and what awareness of one's uniqueness will mean for them.

Typical Guardian Responses

Many Guardians will often cite the major passages that all people go through in life - from the first day at elementary school to marriage and retirement - as well as any concrete factors such as physical handicaps, life ailments, and great pain and suffering that people have to overcome in order to achieve what they have. The way people learn to deal with the entanglements of life is a skill, and that skill was and is valuable to them and makes them unique. Guardians consider these to be signposts of character in others as well as in themselves.

WHAT MAKES YOU UNIQUE?

Typical Rational Responses

Many Rationals concentrate on improving competencies more than anyone else, and a Rational may have a lot of them—some very specific and esoteric—so it is difficult to just settle on one or two aspects and say "that makes me unique." It's about expertise and mastery. How do their abilities, in combination with what they do, provide them with a unique understanding of their area as well as the world and the applications that come from that understanding. Who they are and their character is inseparable from how they do what they do. The Rational quip, "What makes me unique is my DNA!"

Typical Artisan Responses

Many Artisans often think of what they've made of themselves. For example, if an outgoing Artisan has made a network of social links because he or she has the unique skill of winning people over with a charismatic personality, then that's something that makes him or her unique. It's about having their act together as well as a blend or variety of different abilities and characteristics, including any impact they've made. And if they or someone else can do something that others would not succeed at because of lack of effort or fear, then that points to character and is valuable and deserves respect.

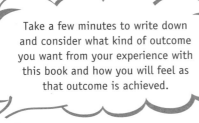

Take a few minutes to write down and consider what kind of outcome you want from your experience with this book and how you will feel as that outcome is achieved.

Temperament In Action

How does temperament play out in everyday life? An Artisan friend and recent college graduate turned down a number of high-paying job opportunities. I asked her why, and she said she craved an enjoyable environment and freedom for life outside work. To no one's surprise, she has successfully jumped into business for herself. She says it's a lot more exciting and makes an impact her own way. A Guardian friend of the family has been working at the same company for thirty years, sometimes putting in fifty to sixty hours a week, travelling often. He explains it hasn't always been easy, but it provides the sense of security and continuity and steps for advancement that he needs and values. Now he is enjoying the early retirement he planned on. My Rational colleague is constantly doing design work on potential new projects and generating new ideas even though she's beleaguered with day-to-day details. The "extra" work allows her to reduce existing stress by making sure her temperament needs are met. And an Idealist friend hasn't "worked" in months. The indifference and devaluing of employees he finds in most jobs violate his values. Instead, he has spent time with his family and time preparing himself for his heart's desire. Now he's on his way to the life he only imagined a few years before.

Choosing Your Temperament

Ranking the temperaments in order of preference is a quick way to define your personal "flavor." Experience also suggests the order of ranking says something about one's path of development. People who identify with the same temperament as most like them but rank the others differently often look and feel quite different from each other. Many people find it easier to rank one temperament as a last choice, then to select one as the temperament they "could not live without." Think about which themes came into your awareness at different periods in your life. Now go back and review temperament in terms of intelligence, needs and values, and stress, and rank them in the box to the right.

Your Compass

Ideally, face-to-face dialogue and feedback with a professional facilitator is needed to tap one's temperament. Remember, although it is believed that personality type is inborn, one's *true self* is often masked by one's *developed self*—family, school and other environmental pressures that often steer us in other directions. We may end up seeing only what others want us to see through their lenses. A part of defining yourself here is asking others how they see you. Similarly, everyone has access to a variety of talents and can see the importance of different values. Sometimes one situation calls for one part of ourselves while other situations call for something different—this is our *contextual self*. This is like looking at ourselves from the outside in. So consider all three aspects of yourself as you continue.

As you start your journey, think of the four ranked temperaments as your compass—a simple framework—to help you keep track of where each piece fits for you and why.

CHOOSING *YOUR* TEMPERAMENT PATTERN
1—Most Like You   2—Somewhat Like You
3—Could Live Without   4—Least Like You

IDEALIST
Search for interpersonal significance and meaning in life's events. Desire to be ethical and authentic in their words and actions. Possess a talent for diplomacy and inspiring language for the future. Respect and encourage the unique identity of each person.

GUARDIAN
Search for the safe security of tradition as they weather life's passages. Desire responsibility and the structures needed to carry out their roles. Possess a talent for logistics and customary ways drawing on the past. Respect and encourage membership and belonging.

RATIONAL
Search for universal concepts and knowledge in life. Desire to further progress—their own or others'. Possess a talent for logical thought and strategically applying ideas in a universal way. Respect and encourage self-mastery and competence in all areas.

ARTISAN
Search for variety, and adapt to the needs of the moment in life. Desire the freedom to act as the situation demands, living in the present. Possess a talent for tactical actions and seeing people's motives. Respect and encourage jumping in and making an impact.

> "Every (crossroads in life) raises its own questions, and the questions... can be answered only by you."
> —Isabel Briggs Myers

Spheres of Life

Life-Themes

"What can I be doing with the rest of my life?" isn't just a question for recent college graduates. Every choice we make about our careers, our family and ourselves is a choice about where we are going with the rest of our lives.

Let's look at John: John has a difficult choice. As a psychologist, he has seen patients in his home office for many years. That's very personal and growth oriented for him and allows him to stay close to his wife and two sons. John has also moved into designing training and teamwork programs for small to midsized companies. That detracts from his individual work but is a way to "reach out" to the community and assist others with similar interests - this appeals to the progressive side of his personal philosophy. A big opportunity recently came along - the chance to work exclusively with large companies for large amounts of money. The entrepreneurial path and its lone-wolf success-oriented philosophy beckons, and this new window of opportunity may soon close. But it will draw him away from his family. What should John do?

John identifies with Rational. Thus, one question is which path of his three options, or combination thereof, best meets his Rational temperament needs and values (knowledge, competence, progress) and is best suited to his Rational talents (strategy, design, theorizing)?

There is another question. To many people, John looks like an Idealist. Why? Idealist needs and values are also important to him. What values would he rank last? What could he live without if he had to or not live without?

▼ C H A R A C T E R ▼

Character, as life-theme: Let's explore the many stories, beliefs, roles and scripts that people live out. Our stories help give meaning to our lives, present us with choices and challenge us to grow.

To help us answer these questions, in the next few pages we will look at eight life-themes that are common to our age and time and place in history. Each life-theme imparts to us a particular look and feel and encourages a set of attitudes and beliefs that sustain that life-theme's "culture." Think of life-themes as "places" we can visit or even immerse ourselves in. They are not just about what we do but how and why. What is your life-theme?

The Life-Themes

- Physical
- Creative
- Establishment
- Community
- Academic
- Entrepreneurial
- Political
- Growth

Life-themes Are Worlds, Not Skill Sets

Someone with technical computer skills can find a home in different places. Here are a few examples:

Physical: Incorporating computer tracking or analysis in sports training.
Artistic: Using technology as a new way to do one's art or to promote art.
Establishment: Computer programming in a large, traditional corporate environment.
Community: Using technology to help bring people together, perhaps in a school setting or for the elderly.
Academic: Training others, using technical skills to do research and to develop and test ideas.
Entrepreneurial: Selling your expertise or computer products.
Political: Using the Internet to give a voice and provide a connection to democracy for millions worldwide.
Growth: Expanding your horizons with a new skill.

Anyone may have been born with gifts in a particular life-theme or have grown up in a family that encouraged a particular one, or perhaps we have chosen consciously to immerse ourselves for one reason or another. Our life-themes will tell us a lot about why some temperament patterns are so attractive to us while others are not, and what we can do about our lives to fulfill our needs and values in terms of balancing both work and relationships.

NOTE:

If you've scored a particular way on a psychological inventory like the MBTI or self-identified with a certain temperament before, you may want to make this an opportunity to re-examine and possibly reconsider what fits you best.

Physical Life-Theme

The outdoors and nature, the world of professional sports, and anything with a focus on the physical, from travel to manual labor, are included. People here often look like Artisans with either a calm and focused or a competitive and energized demeanor. The more a person lives this life-theme for its own sake–and the less a sport or activity is done out of routine or for practice or as a hobby–the more Artisan the person will appear. Because of the common emphasis on confidence, performance, and winning, "success-oriented" attitudes and beliefs are also often stressed, although not necessarily. This life-theme often requires a concrete mind-set and way of life.

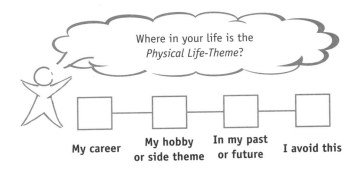

Where in your life is the *Physical Life-Theme*?

| My career | My hobby or side theme | In my past or future | I avoid this |

Most people have some physical outlets but not everyone makes a career here. For the Artisan, whatever the specific area, that area is an end in and of itself. Such Artisans enjoy running, for example, for the sheer pleasure of it or winning for the pleasure of success. They play as long as they feel the impulse to play, and then they stop. A Guardian will be more deterministic and planning–the sport is a task, the object is to win fairly, and there is a right way and a wrong way to play. Rationals here will stress mastery and improvement in abilities–even if the sport starts as a hobby to relax, there is an inner push to make it something more and to enjoy learning. And Idealists will enjoy the team spirit, the communing with nature, or the playing out of a story that they see themselves living.

Mary, now retired, was a swimming instructor for many years. She worked hard, worked-out hard, and had a set training routine for her students. She taught them the philosophy, "challenge yourself, challenge others, and win." She still spends a lot of her time outdoors. Although Mary is a Guardian, many people mistake her and her philosophy as more Artisan. Most of her friends and her husband are Artisans.

Pitfalls: A purely concrete mindset can lead to an impoverished inner life. The next game, the winning scores, the newest training technique–a lifetime of these details may add up to little or leave one closed to life's complexity, or with little to do when the body wears out. A solution is focusing on training the mind as well as the body.

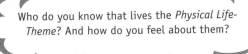

Who do you know that lives the *Physical Life-Theme*? And how do you feel about them?

Can you picture yourself in this life-theme? If you find yourself here, who or what was a catalyst to move you into this theme? If you can't picture yourself, what repulses you?

Creative Life-Theme

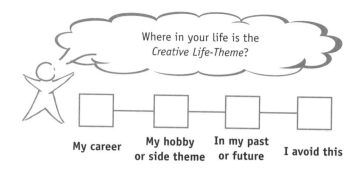

Where in your life is the *Creative Life-Theme*?

My career | **My hobby or side theme** | **In my past or future** | **I avoid this**

The world of the arts—including art, music, crafts, fashion and drama—and anything emphasizing aesthetics and conveying the human element are included. People here often look like Artisans with a relaxed yet enthusiastic or moody and engrossed demeanor. The more spontaneous, concrete and variety oriented–and the more a person does art for its own sake–the more Artisan the person will appear. Because the art world often emphasizes alternative approaches and the creative process, it also often encourages counter cultural or "unconventional" attitudes and beliefs. This life-theme often requires an emotive mind set and way of life.

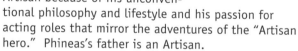

Phineas is an actor. He believes in the human element and "living in the moment" whether on the literal stage or on the stage of life. Although Phineas is an Idealist, he is often mistaken for an Artisan because of his unconventional philosophy and lifestyle and his passion for acting roles that mirror the adventures of the "Artisan hero." Phineas's father is an Artisan.

Creativity has different meanings to different people. For the Artisan here, creativity means composing, performing, creating, or doing something that makes an impact and expresses a personal style. For Idealists in this life-theme, creativity emphasizes the other end of the creative process: inspiring, conveying meaning, expressing intuitive insights and helping people to acknowledge a truth. Rationals here most often stress perfect execution, as well as innovation, originality and abstract methodology–creativity is work. For a Guardian, creativity means those areas traditionally associated with creativity, such as art or music, and becoming creative requires a good mentor and knowledge of correct technique. For the Rational or Idealist, almost anything can be considered creative.

Pitfalls: Each creative subculture has its own rites, expressions and taboos: punk rock and classical ballet do not mix well! The danger lies in pretentiousness and elitism at one end and antisocial isolation at the other. Balance can come with attending to both technique and inner feeling, quality, and reward.

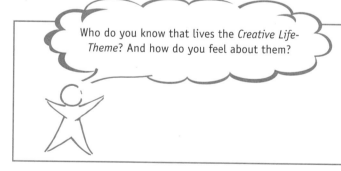

Who do you know that lives the *Creative Life-Theme*? And how do you feel about them?

Can you picture yourself in this life-theme? If you find yourself here, who or what was a catalyst to move you into this theme? If you can't picture yourself, what repulses you?

Establishment Life-Theme

Life here includes the corporate world, traditional institutions or big business, industry, law enforcement, military life, the legal profession, or anything big or establishment. People here often look like Guardians with a serious and matter-of-fact or follow-the-rules demeanor. The establishment often has history and protocols to follow. The more conservative, procedural, and bureaucratic, the more Guardian a person will appear. Because of the establishment's emphasis on rules and regulations, hierarchy and tradition, it often encourages "conventional" attitudes and beliefs. This life-theme often requires a structured mind set and way of life.

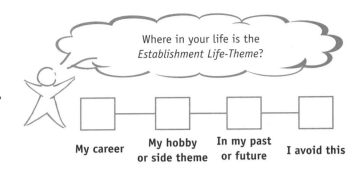

Where in your life is the *Establishment Life-Theme*?

My career | My hobby or side theme | In my past or future | I avoid this

Paul was an engineer in the military and is now a private investigator. He liked the military because of the opportunities it gave him to design, test and improve high-technology equipment. Although Paul is a Rational, he has worked and lived in a large institution and also comes from a traditional family, making him look and feel more Guardian. His wife is a Guardian and so were his father and brothers.

Everyone has to deal with the establishment sometime. The Guardian living this life-theme is the classic traditional, conservative Guardian. He or she may be status quo or efficiency and improvement oriented. Many Artisans here try their best to fit the institutional mold and often make their success within the institution a personal challenge. Idealists are usually here because of the people. If the human element is missing they will flee to another theme. Rationals in this life-theme also often appear Guardian-like but with a strategic and possibly technical edge. Either they believe in their ability to improve the institution at a systemic level, or they stay because they perceive opportunities that only large institutions can provide, to make their personal vision happen.

Pitfalls: While institutions can reach many people, the danger is in treating people as interchangeable widgets. People are ultimately more important than rules. Rules are artificial guides and can be misused to hide from responsible decision making or justify unethical behavior. Institutions are called to tailor themselves to the individual.

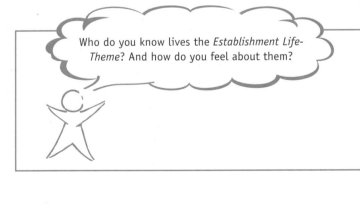

Who do you know lives the *Establishment Life-Theme*? And how do you feel about them?

Can you picture yourself in this life-theme? If you find yourself here, who or what was a catalyst to move you into this theme? If you can't picture yourself, what repulses you?

Community Life-Theme

A life that focuses on the family, local community involvement, charity and volunteerism, children and teens, and anything that has a local or family feel to it is included. People here often look like Guardians with a serious yet kind or lets-all-get-along demeanor. The more everyday, help-oriented, or small-town, the more Guardian a person will appear. Because of the emphasis on being helpful and contributing while maintaining a safe and mutually congenial atmosphere, "participative" attitudes and beliefs are also encouraged. This life-theme often requires an affiliative mind set and way of life.

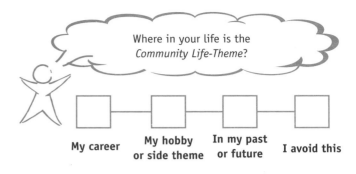

Where in your life is the *Community Life-Theme*?

My career	My hobby or side theme	In my past or future	I avoid this

Almost everyone has family, but family isn't the main attraction for everyone. Guardians here take all the details of volunteerism, community and family very seriously–it is their civic responsibility. Which community they identify with varies individually. Some Guardians spend more time volunteering than they do with their own family! Artisans involved with their community have probably become involved because of someone they already know, motivating personal circumstances, or a crisis situation in which they jumped in to help. Rationals here either grew up with this life-theme, perhaps isolated from other themes, or they may have made a conscious choice to direct their expertise and vision of change here. Idealists with this life-theme will often be here because of their strong beliefs regarding family or community.

Jerome manages a family of four and volunteers in the local community. He has become involved recently with the PTA in chartering and designing a countywide ethics program for the school system. Although Jerome is an Idealist, his small-town upbringing, focus on daily concerns, and volunteerism give him a more Guardian appearance. Jerome had a small-town Guardian schooling.

Pitfalls: A community can become parochial or xenophobic, and just because one has local face-to-face experiece does not mean that outside solutions are unworkable. Small-town caring is not everyone's calling to happiness. Rather, we are all called at least once in life to leave the cradle called home.

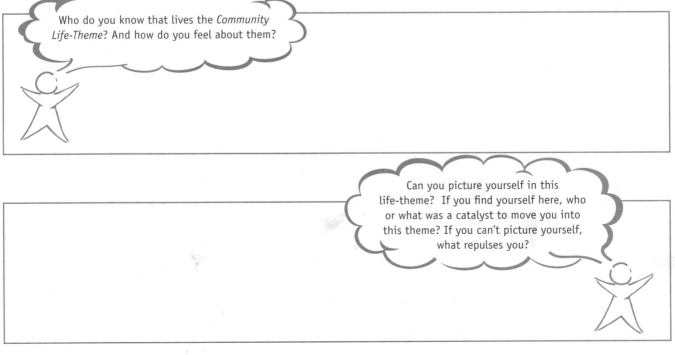

Who do you know that lives the *Community Life-Theme*? And how do you feel about them?

Can you picture yourself in this life-theme? If you find yourself here, who or what was a catalyst to move you into this theme? If you can't picture yourself, what repulses you?

Academic Life-Theme

Academic life refers to teaching, training, scholarship, research, and anything that emphasizes the life of the mind, including education and knowledge for its own sake. People here often look like Rationals, with a demeanor that reflects their emphasis on study, design, and development. The more scientific, rigorous, or technical, the more Rational a person will appear. Even "softer" disciplines have a rich and elaborate language of discourse. Because of the intellectual and skeptical "meta" position that education and academia take on subject matter, "existential" attitudes and beliefs are tacitly encouraged. This life-theme often requires an abstract mind set and way of life.

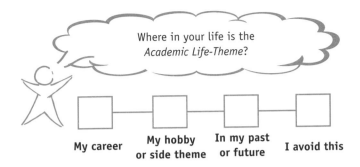

Where in your life is the *Academic Life-Theme*?

My career — **My hobby or side theme** — **In my past or future** — **I avoid this**

Amelia is an anthropologist, social worker and professor. She has published many papers and is well known, but most enjoys getting out into the field and experiencing something new. Although Amelia is an Artisan, her academic background, scientific vocabulary, and experimental approach give her a Rational look and feel. To no surprise, her best friend and her mentor are both Rationals.

Education, knowledge and learning are strongly emphasized today as essential for everyone. To Rationals here, academic life can be an end in itself, a way to develop ideas and technologies in an environment that encourages their goals and provides logistical support. For Idealists in this life-theme, academic life is more about values. Many Idealists are drawn to teaching as part of the larger picture of their life's mission. For this kind of Guardian, academic life is often a challenging and concretely rewarding career path. Artisans who have embraced the academic life-theme often do so because the topic captures them—art, business, computers—and because of the opportunities and experiences their field offers. Mentoring often accompanies the academic theme for all types.

Pitfalls: An ivory-tower mentality can isolate "academe" from the real world. Theory becomes detached from application, and feedback comes only from one's peers. Cynicism replaces creativity. Solutions include interdisciplinary approaches, experimentation, and openess to a genuine joy of teaching.

Who do you know that lives the *Academic Life-Theme*? And how do you feel about them?

Can you picture yourself in this life-theme? If you find yourself here, who or what was a catalyst to move you into this theme? If you can't picture yourself, what repulses you?

Entrepreneurial Life-Theme

This theme includes the Jack of all trades. Anything that involves selling one's skills or turning something innovative and creative into a business, project or product is also included. Today, this often demands comfort with computers and technology, and technical skills often go hand-in-hand with people skills. These people often look like Rationals, with a visionary and realistic or lone-wolf demeanor. The more cutting-edge, esoteric or long term the work is, the more Rational a person will appear. Because of the emphasis on working alone or going one's own way, "independent" attitudes and beliefs are encouraged. This life-theme often requires a pragmatic mind set and way of life.

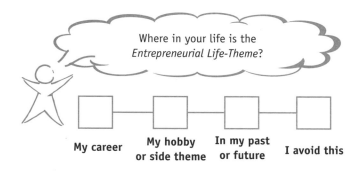

Where in your life is the *Entrepreneurial Life-Theme*?

My career | My hobby or side theme | In my past or future | I avoid this

Madeline is trained as an engineer and now runs her own Internet-based education business. She says she has a lot of fun "wiring herself up" and turning her vague ideas into something nice with commercial appeal. Although Madeline is an Idealist, her background, vocabulary, and strategic mindset give her a Rational look and feel. Her husband and most of her employees are Rationals.

Why not be your own boss? While many Rationals might like to run their own businesses, and entrepreneurs often appear to be like Rationals, the multidisciplinary life of the entrepreneur can be demanding. Rationals here like the autonomy, long-term strategizing and complexity required. Artisans here enjoy the by-the-seat-of-their-pants decision making and rewards of freedom of a self-made life. Many Artisans make outstanding entrepreneurs. For an Idealist, entrepreneurship is often part of a bigger picture about who they are, the purpose of their life, and how to best actualize their contributions. For Guardians who get involved in the entrepreneurial life-theme, it usually matters less what business they are in and more the kind of pay and perks it provides.

Pitfalls: The entrepreneurial life can quickly mean no life at all outside work. Or, without a moral compass, the desire for a quick profit leads to shoddy quality and copycat performance instead of innovation. One solution is to heed the call to ethical and social responsibility and a long-term perspective.

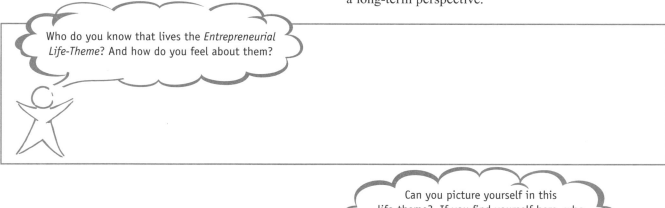

Who do you know that lives the *Entrepreneurial Life-Theme*? And how do you feel about them?

Can you picture yourself in this life-theme? If you find yourself here, who or what was a catalyst to move you into this theme? If you can't picture yourself, what repulses you?

Political Life-Theme

Public life, politics, and anything that has an ideological, proactively religious or activist frame around it are included. People here often look like Idealists, with an evangelistic, politically charged and aware or monastic demeanor. The more change-, people-, or rights-oriented, the more Idealist the person will appear. Because of the emphasis on the expression, maintenance, defense and spreading of values, "empowerment" attitudes and beliefs are often encouraged. "The group" and its ideology may largely define an individual. Thus, this life-theme often requires a collectivist mind set and way of life.

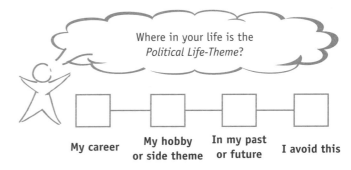

Where in your life is the *Political Life-Theme*?

My career | My hobby or side theme | In my past or future | I avoid this

Someone once said that everything is politics. For Idealists here, a politically active life is about transmitting their beliefs, needs, and values in a way that can change the world and bring happiness to everyone. The paradox here is in using the system for change or bringing about change one person at a time. Political Rationals think globally and often very long term, with an eye on checks and balances and independence in a system. Rationals may also see politics as an avenue for power. Artisans in the political world are often very good to their constituents and make impactful negotiators and charismatic leaders. The norms and sanctioning needs of Guardians here may mean either conservative or liberal politics–they are loyal to the values and culture they grew up with or have committed themselves to, whatever those might be.

Saul is a four-term congressman. He believes in preserving the best of society while improving life for people for the future, and his slogan is "a global vision." Although Saul is a Guardian, his international job position, political philosophy, and change-oriented campaign rhetoric give him an Idealist look and feel. Paul's strongest supporters and henchmen are Idealists.

Pitfalls: The ideology of the group can erase the unique personality of the individual, and scare tactics can close off opportunities for change. A guru's dogma may replace thinking, and the ends may come to justify the means. A solution is a focus on individual gifts in service of the group ideology.

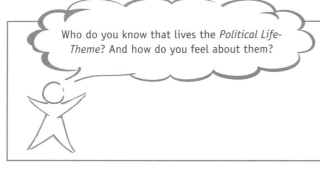

Who do you know that lives the *Political Life-Theme*? And how do you feel about them?

Can you picture yourself in this life-theme? If you find yourself here, who or what was a catalyst to move you into this theme? If you can't picture yourself, what repulses you?

Growth Life-Theme

Counseling, health, psychology, human resources, and anything that is one-on-one or has a personal growth and an apolitical human-issues flavor to it, including spiritual interests and self-improvement, are included. People here often look like Idealists, with an insightful and facilitative demeanor. The more one-on-one, spiritual or mystical, or "potential" oriented, the more Idealist a person will appear. Because of the emphasis on the individual, "self-change and self-awareness" attitudes and beliefs are often encouraged. Individuals here largely define themselves regardless of their culture. Thus, this life-theme often requires an individualistic mind set and way of life.

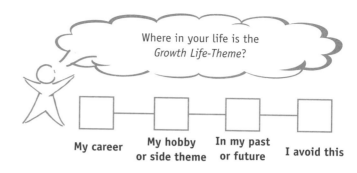

Where in your life is the *Growth Life-Theme?*

My career	My hobby or side theme	In my past or future	I avoid this

Marilyn is a psychologist with her own private practice. She has become bored in the last year and has turned to doing team-training programs for companies. Although Marilyn is an Artisan, her interests, philosophy, and vocabulary come out of her experience as a therapist, making her look and feel more like an Idealist. The ideas that inspire her approach the most are from an Idealist.

Many people today are interested in personal growth. The Idealist who lives this life-theme is probably more adamant than others that the whole point of being alive is self-discovery and self-actualization. For the Rational here, self-actualization means new skills and abilities, including being competent in all eight life-themes! Guardians who focus on growth often equate it with material success in the real world or doing good works and being responsible in all roles in life. They learn from experience and hindsight as they move from graduation and getting a job to child rearing and passing on wisdom. For Artisans in this life-theme, growth is not a set path. It's about the personal experiences they've had that lead them to realize what is really important about living.

Pitfalls: Self-absorption is one way to "get lost" in personal growth. Because one has been in therapy or had a major realization does not mean an end to change—even as we change we remain the same. True spiritual insight is also compassionate and humble! Continuing differences and conflict with others call us to change.

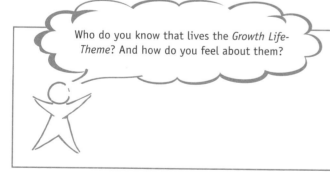

Who do you know that lives the *Growth Life-Theme?* And how do you feel about them?

Can you picture yourself in this life-theme? If you find yourself here, who or what was a catalyst to move you into this theme? If you can't picture yourself, what repulses you?

Finding Balance

As you explore, it is natural to identify with multiple life-themes. Some themes come out of our past, even childhood dreams, while others beckon from around the corner. What is the history behind your life-themes? Family guidance? Self-motivated aspiration? Happenstance? The life-themes illuminate values, roles, mindset, and motivation. Even when conflicted about a career, people often find direction through a philosophical lens.

Let's take a look at John again:
Remember John, our Idealist-looking Rational psychologist? He felt he had to choose between three themes in his life: growth, community, and entrepreneurship. The Entrepreneurial Life-Theme by itself feels too cutthroat and sterile for his taste, while the Growth Life-Theme, all by itself, feels too isolated and intense for him right now. It is the Community Life-Theme–a middle road for him–that energizes him most by providing just the right environment to meet his Rational needs and values.

People often find their best success when one theme is based on their talent as a strong foundation. Then a second theme reflects their interests to keep themselves motivated, and a third can represent a real challenge area to help them keep growing. Write down some of the choices you've had to make between different life-themes.

It's Your Turn

Pick three themes that are the most important to you. They may or may not be a part of your life right now, although they will probably reflect values, attitudes, and beliefs that are important to you.

The Life-Themes

○ **Physical**   ○ **Academic**

○ **Creative**   ○ **Entrepreneurial**

○ **Establishment**   ○ **Political**

○ **Community**   ○ **Growth**

Now that you've had a chance to explore what themes are important to you, take a moment to reflect on the career, family, and personal choices you've made and are currently facing. Keep in mind that each theme often encourages a different philosophy– "empowerment," "success oriented," "self-aware," "existential" and so on. What can you live with? And what is a middle road for you? Living with more than three life-themes can be exhausting and unproductive. Finally, choices are not made just once for all time. Every day we return to what is important to us, choosing again the multiple paths we are on.

▼ C H A R A C T E R ▼

Character is something we are called to actively cultivate. It is an on-going process of choices and changes.

Patterns in Personality

From Four Temperaments to Sixteen Types*

Each of the four temperaments further differentiates into four more personality type patterns, for sixteen types total. Each of these sixteen types displays the core needs and values, talents, and behaviors of the temperament it belongs to, as well its own unique set of interrelated themes.

What Is *Best-Fit Type?*

Best-fit type refers to the type pattern that fits you best. No one description or pattern will be a perfect match to all of who you are. Your personality is rich and complex, and a "type" or type pattern cannot adequately express all of that richness. Each of the sixteen types comes in a variety of "flavors," and *best-fit type* means that the themes and preferred processes of that type seem to fit you the best.

Type is a deep organizing principle within. It is not about external behavior. All of us have access to a multitude of options. Rather, true type is hidden at our core. Sometimes we are tempted to talk about how we can "see" a person's type in his or her observable traits and specific mannerisms, with the belief that a person's true colors show through outward actions. We may be puzzled when people do not "act like" their type or when they act like another type. However, just as we cannot know the true age and character of a tree unless we chop it down, so too can one's true type only be inferred. It lies beneath the surface and one step ahead of our awareness, orchestrating the needed behaviors, life-themes, and cognitive processes that fulfill our core temperament needs and values and type themes.

Sometimes life events and the environment are so counter to a person's core needs and values that exploration is needed to reorient oneself and come closer to rediscovering one's true type. One opportunity for this is when we find it easy to locate others on the type map but cannot seem to find a coherent picture of ourselves. Other times, with maturity, the many flavors and life-themes possible for each type illuminate how we've grown outside the "box" of our type. Thus, type is not a box but a core from which we can grow.

Finally, the themes within each type are interrelated, thus we refer to "type patterns" as opposed to static "types." As you read, pay less attention to the meaning of individual words and phrases and more

attention to the overall pattern the themes of each type imply, taken together. (For example, the theme "communicate and share values" may suggest several scenarios, but when taken together with themes like "reconcile the past with the future" and "intuitive intellect," a particular kind of insightful, empathic and self-disclosing communication process is implied.)

Understanding Your Type Pattern

When we describe a tree, we might talk about roots, a trunk, branches, and leaves, but this does not convey the true sense of "tree-ness." To begin to capture the essense of the tree, we must consider how each part of the tree connects to other parts, what purpose each serves, how the tree's blueprint is contained in its seed, types of trees, the role of trees in the environment, and so on. Even then, no matter how much we say, a dictionary definition of trees may feel flat to us–which does not mean the definition is inaccurate or not useful. To the contrary! Simply, we must go out and experience many real trees in addition to gaining a scientific understanding in order to fully appreciate and comprehend their role.

**Because of your *true self*
you are you and not somebody else.**

A Word about Words!

On the following page, we have chosen various words to try to capture the essence of the themes of each type pattern. These words often reflect the way people with this type pattern think of themselves as well as the deep theoretical underpinnings. However, words are subject to individual interpretations with various connotations, so beware the one-word category! One or two words cannot capture the whole of a pattern. The words were tested with many people, but they are not the last word! Don't let the meaning you may find in any one word or phrase prevent you from considering the pattern as a whole.

> **NOTE:**
>
> If you have completed the MBTI or other personality type instrument, then you may already have some familiarity with the idea of 16 personality type patterns. However, paper-and-pencil measures of personality may or may not be accurate for you. They are single data points only. Many times people end up answering the questions asked in terms of their work, social, or family environment only. As you read through the biographical character sketches, stay open to other possibilities as a best fit for you.

---

* The *Themes* on p.20 and *Snapshots* on pgs. 22–52 are taken from Linda V. Berens and Dario Nardi, *The 16 Personality Types: Descriptions for Self-Discovery*, (Huntington Beach, CA: Telos Publications, 1999)

Patterns in Personality

Themes of the Sixteen Personality Types

The unique themes within each type are inter-related and mutually enriching

FORESEER DEVELOPER
INFJ
Personal growth. Sustain the vision. Honoring the gifts of others. Taking a creative approach to life. Talent for foreseeing. Exploring issues. Bridge differences and connect people. Practical problem solving. Live with a sense of purpose. Living an idealistic life often presents them with a great deal of stress and a need to withdraw.

HARMONIZER CLARIFIER
INFP
Going with the flow. Knowing what is behind what is said. Uncovering mysteries. Exploring moral questions. Talent for facilitative listening. Relate through stories and metaphors. Balancing opposites. Getting reacquainted with themselves. Have a way of knowing what is believable. Struggling with structure and getting their lives in order.

PLANNER INSPECTOR
ISTJ
Drawing up plans and being prepared. Take responsibility. Getting work done first. Being active in the community. Loyalty to their roles. Cultivating good qualities. Doing the right thing. Bear life's burdens and overcome adversity. Talented at planning, sequencing, and noticing what's missing. Having to learn so much in hindsight is painful at times.

PROTECTOR SUPPORTER
ISFJ
Noticing what's needed and what's valuable. Talent for careful and supportive organization. Know the ins and outs. Enjoy traditions. Work to protect the future. Listening and remembering. Being nice and agreeable. Unselfish willingness to volunteer. Feeling a sense of accomplishment. Exasperated when people ignore rules and don't get along.

IDEALIST THEMES | **GUARDIAN THEMES**

ENVISIONER MENTOR
ENFJ
Communicate and share values. Succeeding at relationships. Realizing dreams—their own and others. Seek opportunities to grow together. Heeding the call to a life work or mission. Enjoy the creative process. Intuitive intellect. Reconcile the past and the future. Talent for seeing potential in others. Often find living in the present difficult.

DISCOVERER ADVOCATE
ENFP
Inspiring and facilitating others. Exploring perceptions. Talent for seeing what's not being said and voicing unspoken meanings. Seek to have ideal relationships. Recognize happiness. Living out stories. Want to authentically live with themselves. Respond to insights in the creative process. Finding the magical situation. Restless hunger for discovering their direction.

IMPLEMENTOR SUPERVISOR
ESTJ
Talent for bringing order to chaotic situations. Educating themselves. Industrious, work-hard attitude. Balance work with play. Having a philosophy of life. Having the steps to success. Keeping up traditions. Being well balanced. Connecting their wealth of life experiences. Often disappointed when perfectionistic standards for economy and quality are not met.

FACILITATOR CARETAKER
ESFJ
Accepting and helping others. Managing people. Hearing people out. Voicing concerns and accommodating needs. Admire the success of others. Remember what's important. Talented at providing others with what they need. Keep things pleasant. Maintaining a sense of continuity. Accounting for the costs. Often disappointed by entrepreneurial projects.

CONCEPTUALIZER DIRECTOR
INTJ
Maximizing achievements. Drive for self-mastery. Build a vision. Very long-range strategizing. Realizing progress toward goals. Systems thinking. Talent for seeing the reasons behind things. Being on the leading edge. Maintaining independence. Find it difficult to let go in interacting with others.

DESIGNER THEORIZER
INTP
Becoming an expert. Seeing new patterns and elegant connections. Talent for design and redesign. Crossing the artificial boundaries of thought. Activate the imagination. Clarifying and defining. Making discoveries. Reflect on the process of thinking itself. Detach to analyze. Struggle with attending to the physical world.

ANALYZER OPERATOR
ISTP
Actively solving problems. Observing how things work. Talent for using tools for the best approach. Need to be independent. Act on their hunches or intuitions. Understanding a situation. Taking things apart. Making discoveries. Sharing those discoveries. Unsettled by powerful emotional experiences.

COMPOSER PRODUCER
ISFP
Taking advantage of opportunities. Stick with what's important. Talent for pulling together what is just right. Creative problem solving. Building relationships. Attracting the loyalties of others. Being their own true self. Have their own personal style. Play against expectations. Struggle with nurturing their own self-esteem.

RATIONAL THEMES | **ARTISAN THEMES**

STRATEGIST MOBILIZER
ENTJ
Being a leader. Maximize talents. Marshal resources toward progress. Intuitive explorations. Forging partnerships. Mentoring and empowering. Talent for coordinating multiple projects. Balance peace and conflict. Predictive creativity. Often overwhelmed by managing all the details of time and resources.

EXPLORER INVENTOR
ENTP
Being inventive. Talented at building prototypes and getting projects launched. Lifelong learning. Enjoy the creative process. Share their insights about life's possibilities. Strategically formulate success. An inviting host. Like the drama of the give and take. Trying to be diplomatic. Surprised when their strategizing of relationships becomes problematic.

PROMOTER EXECUTOR
ESTP
Taking charge of situations. Tactical prioritizing. Talent for negotiating. Want a measure of their success. Keep their options open. Enjoy acting as a consultant. Winning people over. Caring for family and friends. Enjoy exhilaration at the edge. Disappointed when others don't show respect.

MOTIVATOR PRESENTER
ESFP
Stimulating action. Have a sense of style. Talent for presenting things in a useful way. Natural actors—engaging others. Opening up people to possibilities. Respect for freedom. Taking risks. A love of learning, especially about people. Genuine caring. Sometimes misperceive others' intentions.

Helping You Decide

After reviewing the themes on
the facing page, use the matrix below to

• Cross out the ones that are *not like you.*

• Then, of the ones left, check those
that *appeal to you.*

Be sure to think of yourself in all contexts,
not just at work or at home.
Who are you really?

❏ INFJ Page 48	❏ INFP Page 52	❏ ISTJ Page 32	❏ ISFJ Page 36
❏ ENFJ Page 46	❏ ENFP Page 50	❏ ESTJ Page 30	❏ ESFJ Page 34
❏ INTJ Page 40	❏ INTP Page 44	❏ ISTP Page 24	❏ ISFP Page 28
❏ ENTJ Page 38	❏ ENTP Page 42	❏ ESTP Page 22	❏ ESFP Page 26

Character Biographies
for Self-Discovery

Real people are not mere mechanical composites of themes, factors, strategies, values, and traits. Thinking this way is simply a tool for understanding, and each person is an organic "whole system." Seeing people as "wholes" instead of "parts" provides us with a deeper understanding of ourselves and makes it easier to work through the complex choices we have to make, choices that often reflect a multitude of aspects about ourselves, not just one part.

So far we have looked at character in terms of personality patterns and in terms of the life-themes—the stories and roles people live out. Beyond this, character can also refer to uniqueness.

▼ C H A R A C T E R ▼

Character as uniqueness: Temperament informs how we define uniqueness, but it is our quirks, upbringing, and specific set of life experiences that make us unique, apart from everyone else.

Each of the sixty-four biographies presents not just a personality pattern and life-theme, but a unique person and their life.

While people of the same temperament and type have in common certain temperament core needs and values and type themes, there remain many differences such as what sphere of life they work, play, love, and learn in. Everyone is unique and has his or her own character.

Sixty-four biographical character sketches–four for each of the sixteen types–have been developed based on extensive interviews. Each sketch is a character, is written to convey a sense of character, and points to "character" as a developmental pattern. Each sketch is based on multiple people of the same temperament and type and of similar flavor or "character." And each sketch, while written in the third person, incorporates pieces of that individual's language and other idiosyncrasies. The four biographies created for each type represent the diversity of that type– different contexts and developmental paths lead to different shadings of character. Undoubtedly, there are myriad variations within a type–some common, some rare, some stereotypical, some diverse. Only four were included, and thus others left out.

To help you get started, you may want to begin exploring a specific temperament or type. Within each temperament you will find many people. You may resonate with some and not with others. Within each type, only two or three of the four biographies may appeal to you. Suggestions for other characters to look at also accompany each type. As you read, think about who you like and why. Ask yourself what ideal image you have for yourself. What matches with parents, family and friends? And write down any questions you may want to ask yourself–and others–while reading. These questions will help you locate yourself on your map and act as sign posts and tools for the road afterward. Your guided self-discovery process continues on page 54.

Other Suggested Patterns

Our experiences in facilitating self-discovery with thousands of people have led us to suggest that some type patterns can be genuine "look-alikes" in certain contexts. Most often these similarities are based on how people experience the self-discovery process. As you read the biographies, you will find suggestions of other types to look at. If one pattern you select doesn't quite fit then you can use these to guide you in other directions.

Everyone can be a chameleon in context, and different flavors bring home the rich diversity within each type. Every type can be successful in any area.

s
n
a
p
s
h
o
t

Theme is promoting. Talents lie in persuading others and expediting to make things happen. Have an engaging, winning style that others are drawn to. Adept at picking up on minimal nonverbal cues. Anticipate the actions and reactions of others and thus win their confidence. Like the excitement and challenge of negotiating, selling, making deals, arbitrating, and in general, achieving the impossible. Thrive on action and the freedom to use all resources at hand to reach desired outcomes.

Other types to look at: ISTP, ESFP, ESTJ

Promoter Executor
Temperament:
Artisan
Interaction Style:
In Charge
Cognitive Processes:
$S_e T_i F_e N_i$ $S_i T_e F_i N_e$

Ross (Financial Consultant)

In the world of finance and investment, you have to have a handle on what's going on in the marketplace, what's going on with people and what's in it for them. And Ross is a natural. He gets a clear picture of the situation and sets things up for his clients to fix their problems. His law school background helps. And he knows all his clients by name and has that respectful attitude with his coworkers that gets them to follow along. His family knows him as laid-back and hang loose, and he enjoys the good things in life, but he's also just as serious about his goals and taking advantage of opportunities as they come along - just out of school eight years and he's making lots of money. It's a lot like betting at the track, Ross explains: you feel that streak of good luck and want to keep on gambling but you have to know better. He likes to have focus and some kind of plan so he's doing something. Ross collects guns and likes to go hunting and is a volunteer firefighter. His wife worries about him, but he loves the exhilaration of working so close to the edge. Sometimes he takes his sons out hunting. And he's very careful that they have their heads on straight. "It's exciting to watch other people get crazy and do wild stuff," he tells them, "but you have to know what you're doing." He really cares about them and nothing is too good for his family and friends. Ross has a lot of respect for people who do something with their lives, getting themselves "out there." And when people think of that, they think of him.

Kelly (Personal Trainer)

People know Kelly as active and super out-going with a take-charge attitude - a natural athlete and saleswoman and a great negotiator. She has been working on her own initiative and earning money for herself since she was a kid. She supported herself through school teaching aerobics and later earned certification as a personal trainer and sports and fitness consultant. She sees that sports and fitness attract people with money, and this has been important experience toward running her own business. Kelly often ends up in charge of money matters or acting as a financial consultant wherever she works, and she knows how to direct people when she needs to. Sometimes other women complain she is very competitive, and she knows she easily fits in as "one of the guys." People say she could be a professional comedian with all her stories. Kelly's had quite a variety of boyfriends over the years; she likes to take the initiative in approaching men and getting to know them and definitely wants to have a big say in running the relationships. Naturally, she works part time at a number of different jobs and networks with a lot of people because it's important to keep one's options open - she is quick to spot and leap at challenging opportunities and even more skilled at closing deals with people. In her "free time," Kelly paints and goes to art fairs to sell her work. She uses automotive paints to create brilliantly alive, stunning pieces that beg customers to be taken home. She rides a motorcycle and travels the country. Kelly also enjoys playing guitar - which is her quiet time.

Notice and Act:
Write down your reaction, people you know of this type,
questions to ask, values you share with this type.

Lana (French Teacher)

On the face of it, Lana is a quaint retired French teacher. Never mind that she ended up an expatriate in the World War II French resistance and was a professional translator for jungle expeditions and desert wars. Lana has had many interests and objectives over the years; she takes opportunities when they come along and lives life on the edge. She simply keeps her priorities straight, knowing what she's getting into and having certain goals to achieve. How else could she have survived being stranded on a small island in the Indian Ocean for four months? She loves all things French (movies and art, fashion and people) and believes that therein lie beauty and romance. The love of her life saw the world the same way she did, doing the things she relishes. And she felt kind of weird when she discovered there was a kind of person who could tell her all about herself. He made her stop and think twice about why she was here and what the world really means. Luckily, she married him—not that she settled down. As she sees it, she's her own person, giving her own meaning to life with the ideal that one can achieve a lot if one is motivated. Lana says age is in the mind and youth is in the heart. She still travels all over the world, returning to her seaside home between trips to touch base with family. She loves young people, with their enthusiasm and humor, and they hang on her every word when she recounts her true stories of love and adventure.

Andy (Martial Artist)

Andy was born a little guy, but after two tours of duty in the Marine Corps as a sniper, people think twice before getting smart with him. Andy was drawn into the world of martial arts while stationed in the Far East and opened a dojo with the money he saved up; he's been training and competing ever since. Andy's always up at dawn and takes pleasure in waking everyone. Four routine marriages and nine great kids later, he's the undisputed head of his household. He loves spending time with his kids and tells people he would fight anyone or anything for them. He's very protective (especially of his daughters) but gives them the push that they need—no babying them. Andy's own deceased father gets all of his respect and admiration, and when he's feeling down he thinks of how his father fought his way up from nothing and taught him how to stand up for himself. Andy will avenge any disrespect of friends or family. He reasons that in today's world, one has to hold one's own and sees martial arts as a tool, a way to ground himself that he takes very seriously. He tells his students - and his kids are his students too - that while martial arts is intended as peaceful, they should be ready to use it. Ask anyone and they'll say Andy's a nice guy—with a funny if "off-color" sense of humor—the kind who's really good to have as a friend and really terrible to have as an enemy. The police are his friends. They respect the fire that runs in his blood.

Theme is action-driven problem solving. Talents lie in operating all kinds of tools and instruments and using frameworks for solving problems. Keen observers of the environment, they are a storehouse of data and facts relevant to analyzing and solving problems. Thrive on challenging situations and having the freedom to craft clever solutions and do whatever it takes to fix things and make them work. Take pride in their skill and virtuosity, which they seem to effortlessly acquire.

Other types to look at: ESTP, ISTJ, INTJ

Analyzer Operator
Temperament: Artisan
Interaction Style: Chart the Course
Cognitive Processes: $T_i S_e N_i F_e T_e S_i N_e F_i$

Chris (Military Pilot)

Chirs is a fighter pilot, astronaut, and sports and car buff. In high school he fixed cars. He loves to take things apart and figure out how they work and someday wants to be an investigator - taking apart the scene, situation and people and figuring out the events and motives—or a sports instructor. In high school he did wrestling, track, and cross-country. And when Chris gets time off, he shines his car and races it out on the new car test tracks. As a pilot, he also knows aircraft inside and out, the name and function of every part. The military gives great opportunities for adventure and pushing oneself, but he finds the rules stupid sometimes. When the aircraft carrier would stop at foreign ports, he found it interesting to observe if other people enjoyed the same freedoms he has. A buddy was downed and taken hostage once, and Chris has thought out actions he might take in that situation. He sees that once you understand something you can do anything. Independence Day is his favorite holiday. Chris likes jazz. A couple of years ago, Chris was accepted into astronaut training. He's been in space once. It was both exhilarating and mind wrenching. People know him as a very calm, serious, focused guy, but when something really powerful and emotional happens he absorbs the impact of the entire experience with great intensity and detail. Looking out the largest port hole from orbit at the small rotating multi-colored speck that people call Earth - he thinks he feels lucky, one of only a handful of human beings to have that kind of perspective.

Amelia (Anthropologist)

Anthropologist, social worker, educator - Amelia blends her ideals into an active life of exploration and how things relate and evolve. In her writings, she explains how survival and growth mean trial and error plus experimentation and how noticing a question means one is ready to deal with a situation. At conferences, she presents her findings logically; in her own mind, she has a mix of criteria. Amelia can get impatient if things are too academic, likes to do something concrete and immediate for social change, and is most at home with field work: being right here, right now, instead of talking about "over there". That leads to the kind of pioneering work that keeps her interested. She tells the students that there are no mistakes, only learning experiences, and when you leave home, things will be presented to you in various forms, by various people and situations, and these are opportunities to learn important lessons because no part will lack significance. Amelia sees anthropology as both an area of study and as a way to explore personal limits while building one's own life story. She runs workshops for professionals from related disciplines, although when she follows up later she often finds that they are misapplying the ideas and have forgotten the specific signs and patterns she thought she had covered. And some people are too negative to deal with. They have their own agendas. But she trusts that life gives people the tools they need; what they do with those is up to them. "And what you see out there sees you."

Notice and Act:
Write down your reaction, people you know of this type,
questions to ask, values you share with this type.

Karen (Entrepreneur)

Karen's just jumped into her own international business. She has a lot of technical know-how and business experience, having "worked the system" in several positions, and she knows what factors to watch. Business school also gave her the clarity she needed to go it alone - learning the importance of vision and strategic planning. And Karen likes her independence - doing things her own way, by herself, she's easily bored and needs variety. She's very pragmatic. Playing with the "big boys" now takes all of her energy, and sometimes she's ended up redoing or improvising on her own the botched and late projects she's gotten from partner companies. She often feels a drive to keep projects moving and get them out the door because opportunity and the bank and taxes wait for no one. Karen has no problem figuring out what others want and what they're up to. That makes being a CEO easy. It's just that so many people get stuck in the past or on their various issues. Her attitude is; "get over it." She admits that sometimes, with a few people, she has gotten overly attached and sentimental, but she still dates a lot and really likes it when her dates are intelligent and good-looking. Karen loves the rush of the entrepreneurial life and different cultures. She's very competitive, especially with herself and her own standards of progress, and the stakes are a little higher than when she was running cross-country or doing martial arts in high school. Maybe that's why she likes extreme sports. She'd like to think her dogs understand.

Charlie (Veterinarian)

Charlie, or Cheetah Man as he's known, is intense, independent and sure of himself. He is generally quiet but enjoys an audience; his eyes sparkle when he tells anecdotes about cheetahs and Africa. While he is an expert cheetah researcher, he is known for his deep and very genuine love for the animals. He is quick and steady in his movements and a little less certain about people than cheetahs - to cheetahs, he is just another one of them. Charlie dislikes change and surprise, yet he has always avoided following the crowd to make a road of his own. He has traveled the world, observing different cultures and how humans, animals, and the environment relate in complex patterns. On one trip, a Polynesian shaman introduced him to the idea of a spirit world and psychic ability. The experience was very powerful, and he remains interested and intrigued by the flashes of intuitive insight he experiences and how to use his intuition. Charlie tells people that being scared is normal, and if you stop and wonder what to do, you're finished. You have to switch over your thinking, react like an animal. While he travels less now, Charlie returns to nature however he can and tracks the progress of organizations and causes that fight for what he thinks is important. He knows fitness is essential and stays healthy and active. He is also a natural with mechanical devices and works on his classic car in his spare time. Science and the future intrigue him. Charlie is a deeply private person in a genuine sort of way.

Theme is performance. Warm, charming, and witty. Want to impact and help others, to evoke their enjoyment, and to stimulate them to act. Want to make a difference and do something meaningful. Often masterful at showmanship, entertaining, motivating, and presenting. Thrive on social interaction, joyful living, and the challenge of the unknown. Like helping people get what they want and need, facilitating them to get results.

Other types to look at: ISFP, ESTP, ESFJ

Motivator Presenter
Temperament: Artisan
Interaction Style: Get Things Going
Cognitive Processes: $S_e F_i T_e N_i$ $S_i F_e T_i N_e$

Sandy (Entrepreneur)

Sandy is perpetual motion. With many interests and even more acquaintances, she enjoys spending time with friends and going new places. She makes everything a colorful adventure, and people trust her to make things work and make them happen. Sandy has done dozens of jobs and excelled at all of them - she gets bored staying with one job and her freedom comes first. She most enjoyed her Emergency Room work and stint handling a radio crisis hot-line. She also worked in the juvenile court system; the injustice she saw made it the only job that ever really bothered her. She has started her own businesses: a weekend-adventure business, an interior-design company, a modeling agency, and school to promote fresh print and film talent. Sandy has a strong sense of what looks good and is very conscious of her appearance - clothing, makeup, and hair - and the presentation she gives. But no one says she is conceited. She just knows these things are important and takes a no-nonsense attitude. Sensible exercise and a balanced diet are also key to staying healthy and attractive. Sandy dates a lot and doesn't obsess over men - most of her friends are men, and she usually knows what she wants and what they want. And Sandy doesn't take anything for granted and can take situations very personally: she cries at a good film, and when people are joyous or red with anger or in tears or shaking with fear, that moves her. She's aware of how perceptive she is of people's physical behaviors and real desires, but mentioning these perceptions has created problems for her in the past. She tries to see everyone's point of view.

Joel (Musician)

Joel's a natural actor, not just one personality. As he says, people give off a certain energy and some people are comfortable with that energy - they're in synch. That's what he likes about music. It conveys the vibe he wants, often very dramatically. Travel is very pleasurable too, meeting people and basking in the atmosphere of a place, laughing with new friends while trying strange foods and bizarre customs. He grew up in the Caribbean as a missionary child, and with the diversity he's experienced he's found the conventional world limiting and difficult. Joel has sometimes questioned his abilities in the past, but wherever he's been in life, he feels that's okay and worrying doesn't help. Life is not linear. Joel craves stories and jokes and can entertain people for hours. He respects anyone who is genuine and caring and smart, and he really feeds off of the excitement and energy that comes from being at the center of a live crowd. His music just seems like random words and notes dedicated to those he loves, and he's a natural on stage—with the microphone or in front of a camera—and his voice is poetry, sensuous and passionate, the deep feeling of his convictions really comes through in the grace of his voice. Joel respects that everyone is their own person and can do what they want, and sometimes he takes a certain delight in letting annoying people go merrily on their way, telling them what they want to hear while going around them. Politically, Joel's very progressive.

Notice and Act:
Write down your reaction, people you know of this type, questions to ask, values you share with this type.

Kent (Football Player)

The excitement, the cheers of the fans, the drama of the game - Kent just made it to the pros a few years ago and every day is like a party. He tells the kids at the schools he visits, "Don't hold back, enjoy just being alive." And a kid always comes up to him afterwards. He loves to listen and help young people pull out of their problems and get going again, finding their place. Kent hates being alone and gets bored easily, and he has plenty of friends and past girlfriends, but they often limit his freedom. Sometimes his coach is a real stickler too, but he believes you have to have respect for the guy, for his experience and the position he's reached. "You're impulsive, and you lack discipline," Coach once said. That was the time Kent couldn't resist the chance to do a little modeling. Kent doesn't complain and doesn't like to make waves. If he disagrees with someone about something really important, he pretends to agree with the person and then goes off and does what he wants. He married a few months ago; his wife has a son from a previous marriage and he took the boy in as his own. He truly loves the little guy, and the little guy truly loves Kent's drum set. When he gives Kent a hug and closes his eyes or gives that big smile, that shows the depth of emotion. Smooth and entertaining, with a happy face and a generous heart, after lending a friend some money recently, Kent has come to see that he can sometimes be a little too trusting. There's so much fun living left to do. He just wants everything to be wonderful.

Marilyn (Organizational Consultant)

Marilyn just loves helping people; she has a huge desire to help. Her talent is facilitation, although her work involves a good measure of training and consulting in the area of management and performance. She's well known for her dramatic, interactive presentations, how she can evoke humor and make ideas hit home. With customer needs, she asks a lot of questions and can get really excited because it's a lot of fun learning about a whole new area. Marilyn "senses" very well: she perceives if a person is angry or happy inside, whether a person is trying to help or influence her. She respects honesty. She can also be abrasive sometimes - it's her political side - but she's always willing to listen and work with conflicting desires, helping people realize the conflict is just a test. She's amazed that in our world we can't take care of our own people. She feels we should "get in there and just deal with it"; it would feel like a risk not to. Personally, she doesn't like too much change or negativity, and won't play "follow the leader" - she will fight that and believes one needs different leaders at different times. That's her value of independence. Both cynical and optimistic, she prides herself on having a healthy sense of balance and aim for what she wants in life and what's important for her well-being. Marilyn's also a voracious reader, and with all the tools she's learned over the years, she really feels she's been making a contribution, bringing her unique capabilities into acceptance. Sometimes it feels like she's on a mission. What feels great is when everything clicks.

snapshot

Theme is composing, using whatever is at hand to get a harmonious, aesthetic result. Talents lie in combining, varying, and improvising, frequently in the arts but also in business and elsewhere. With their senses keenly tuned in they become totally absorbed in the action of the moment, finding just what fits the situation or the composition. Thrive on having the freedom to vary what they do until they get just the right effect. Take action to help others and demonstrate values. Kind and sensitive to the suffering of others.

Other types to look at: ESFP, ISFJ, INFP

Composer Producer
Temperament: Artisan
Interaction Style: Behind the Scenes
Cognitive Processes: F_i S_e N_i T_e F_e S_i N_e T_i

Lisa (Art Professor)

Lisa's art is her medium for self-expression. She loves the form, movement, and style inherent in living things. She paints, draws, and sculpts the human body, plants, and animals and the everyday objects they encounter in the world. It's all a harmonious variation on a theme, she tells her students. She likes life to be uncomplicated, but the business opportunities for different media using computers really caught her eye recently, and she feels these overpopulating machines need a human touch. Lisa is anything but touchy-feely. She has as strong a sense of fakes and phonies as she does for color, line, and texture, and she hates it when people are irrational and try to force ridiculous rules on others. She believes that people should act natural and have the freedom to get things done however they want to, and she has an endless memory for stories about the weird situations and strange people she's met over the years. Her friends often get the impression that she does what she does to evoke strong reactions from people, but she sees herself as a very private person who just wants to relax and enjoy the nice everyday little things. It is these moments that she loves to capture in her art, as well as the quiet grace and turbulent pulse of life that hides within them. "But then that's part of your own personal sense of beauty," one of her more talented and enchanting students once said to her.

James (Entrepreneur)

Cynical yet optimistic, James believes a life ethic is very important. People trust him to deliver. He can find himself bored when a job is too easy, unless he really cares, then he stays with it. That's probably why he's so dedicated to what he does, which is simply a little of a lot of things that tie people and technology across international boundaries. At heart he's a self-made businessman, not just a CEO, and he equates politics with business, with most people "playing the game." James tells people he likes technology because it makes life easy: to communicate, to advertise, to be creative, to live at the leading edge. And it's good to have something tangible that sells. He doesn't want to risk his family. He strategizes, asks questions, gets information, looks for reasons why and thinks about people's responses. He wants his clients and employees to feel like they have a mutual friendship, and he doesn't want anyone to say honestly that he cheated them. Now that he feels he's made it, with a secluded home, a beautiful view, and the animals and creative comforts, James wants to give back something good that will instill a sense of values. He responds to the big picture - the revelation that there's more to living than what people assume, something rational and fair. He's competitive, especially with himself, and he believes progress comes when you "play it hands off," letting the future emerge by itself. He's so happy to see his children - good kids - going off into an exciting world, he can hardly stand it. Twice James has been voted "Most Valuable Corporate Player."

Notice and Act:
Write down your reaction, people you know of this type,
questions to ask, values you share with this type.

Kurt (Rock Musician)

Kurt is mellow, friendly and down to earth and largely keeps to himself and his friends. Kurt has enjoyed playing music since junior high school. He played music along with doing a lot of other activities in college, where he started his band. He likes his music and is good at it and is becoming like the lead guitarist in his favorite band. Kurt's popular and a lot of people are magically attracted to him; he doesn't know why. His friends are people like himself. He's always happier when he has a girlfriend, but his music comes first. He stresses that a musician's life should always be about the music. Sometimes Kurt reads his poetry and short stories to his girlfriends, and he wants to be able to talk to his friends about his feelings and relationships. He plays sports now and then - he's been playing hockey since he was a small kid - and he loves being on a team. He's always moving from one promising job to the next to support his career and help out his friends. Kurt's loyalty and emotions feel deep and genuine to those around him, but he also gives the impression he is a daring rules-breaker. He enjoys books and movies that play up the life others think he leads, and he loves how characters end up in weird relationships like his own. His friends are often surprised to find him toting around a science fiction book and equally surprised at the creative business strategies he sometimes thinks up. Kurt himself is often surprised at how he attracts animals; they are just like good people to him. Sometimes he can get lost in remembering the whole past and all the people he's known and great times he's had.

Maria (Physical Therapist)

Relaxed, sensual, mystical, innocent, outdoorsy, sweat—these all describe Maria. What's best about being a massage therapist for Maria is that she really enjoys spending time with people. All her clients tell her she is a good listener - she remembers what they say, the details about their lives. She meets a lot of interesting people too. She feels attracted to men who have their lives in order but who aren't too into themselves or mean. Maria lives for romance and can be shy, but she and her best friend double date and they do lots of fun activities together - that makes it easier to deal with toxic people. Maria needs variety and enjoys doing lots of different things, especially outdoors, and finds it hard to concentrate unless she enjoys or cares about something. Often others don't realize when she cares about something and are surprised to find that out about her. She's often willing to go out of her way to please someone important, and naturally she looks out for herself. Maria never pushes herself too hard and takes pleasure in the simple things. She's fashionable in the sense that she has her own style. That's what she enjoyed about tennis for so many years: the challenge with the freedom to display her own style. She likes photography too. She certainly doesn't want to be like everybody else. Mysticism and that level of life really attracts her. Her beliefs here overcome any self-doubts. Maria's at her best when someone comes in with a problem and there is little to work with. Then she can create magic. She loves helping people.

Theme is supervising, with an eye to the traditions and regulations of the group. Responsible, hardworking, and efficient. Interested in ensuring that standards are met, resources conserved, and consequences delivered. Talents lie in bringing order, structure, and completion. Want to keep order so the organization, group, family, or culture will be preserved. Thrive on organizing and following through with commitments and teaching others how to be successful.

Other types to look at: ISTJ, ENTJ, ESTP

Implementor Supervisor
Temperament:
    Guardian
Interaction Style:
    Get Things Going
Cognitive Processes:
    T_e S_i N_e F_i T_i S_e N_i F_e

Mike (Trainers Trainer)

Mike is a human relations consultant and "trainers' trainer." His clients know he cuts through red tape and always has the right resources available for them. His approach to his training material is complete and no-nonsense - it's all a simple system of tried-and-true steps that anyone can be taught to follow. And he's always sure to throw in some fun. His approach to business is also hard-nosed and competitive, and he credits his success to his common sense, winning business background and military experiences. Mike gladly traded four years of military duty for a free college education and found that it was a fantastic way to teach someone a lot. Establishment packaging, a let-live attitude, and a sense of class is what it takes in his book. In college, he majored in philosophy and is still an avid reader. He loves to argue philosophy and politics just for fun. Several times, when life hasn't been too kind, Mike has turned to his basic beliefs, made an analogy to his own life, and then turned the situation around. Chorus and band are favorite hobbies. He often throws formal parties for clients and goes all out for the customary holidays and family get-togethers. Mike strongly believes in his duties as a husband and father and works hard teaching his kids how to be successful in life. Mike met his wife in high school and pursued her the old-fashioned way; he delights in her sense of humor and how they can laugh together doing something fun. It's that kind of relationship that he emphasizes as a trainer.

Jocelyn (Diplomat)

Wife and mother of the household and diplomat for her nation. Jocelyn really enjoys her work. She manages her inheritance, the family estate, and has even turned a profit on the place. She puts it to all sorts of uses, including horseback riding and other social activities for her adolescents and their friends in prep school. She wants nothing but the best. As a diplomat and frequent traveler, she sees those who don't have the necessary tools to deal with their problems and observes how many people, youths in particular, are mixed up and on a truly unfortunate track. Thus it's very relieving to watch her own progeny growing up and taking on their adult roles in life. She will feel the sadness when they leave the nest - Jocelyn herself has a real sentimental streak. Her husband, a famous teaching surgeon, has found more time for family recently, and it has been just wonderful to have him home. Diplomacy, reserve, and a sense of humility are necessary to balance justice with liberties. She especially enjoys closing words—gently "sticking it" to opponents—and how speakers always employ a red-herring to divert the public's attention. She knows people have their elaborate philosophies and try to force them when really it's about what they're getting from others. They want special treatment and when they don't get it they escalate conflict, making it harder on themselves and everyone. She's believes, from her own perspective, what people need is a wealth of experience in life to make the right connections between everything that's important, and when she observes someone's on the right track, she believes it's important to quietly let them know that.

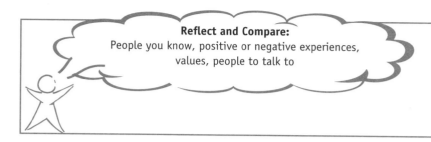

Reflect and Compare:
People you know, positive or negative experiences,
values, people to talk to

Alexandra (Stage Singer)

Alexandra, a professional nightclub singer, loves getting up on stage and doing her routine: from the old favorites to a few charming piano tunes, the right magical effects and a seance to top off the show. Sometimes she really does sense her departed parents. "I just know," she tells people. She and her troupe play mostly to the older and more sophisticated, and it's great when the young people come in. But if you don't pick the classy clubs, she says, "you lose your good reputation." She picks only the best, properly trained musicians and stagehands. Alexandra's a penny pincher and knows how to drive a hard bargain. She gets involved, talking to salespeople and doing her homework when buying equipment - she hates to end up working with less-than-perfect products. It took five years for her custom home to be built and she fired a dozen contractors for shoddy work. It was for her and her daughter. Alexandra's daughter takes after her ex-husband, a famous chess player and mathematician. His genius still confuses her. Alexandra's heritage is very important: she involves her daughter, and it shows in her acts and support of political causes. Some have suggested she run for office, being a real go-getter and so up on the issues. She loves intelligent conversation, and she believes in her beliefs, but she tells her daughter to never get emotionally involved. After all these years, memories of all the good times still bring tears to her eyes.

Brett (Student President)

Brett is a natural leader and determined and doesn't mind making waves. As college student president, he makes himself very clear about his principles and governs himself accordingly. He's very modern, especially about relationships and the like and believes in preserving and enhancing what's good about civilization. He's educated himself about the web of society's institutions and is questioning of how things are done by the establishment and who's doing them. Brett is particularly aware of hierarchy, power, and authority at the university and familiarizes himself with his opponents to show decisiveness in refuting them - the facts and figures, put together in a logical case, and his opponents' own words usually speak for themselves. Besides keeping busy with friends, he tutors, works out, and models for art classes, and he enjoys the excitement of competition and pushing himself, with people cheering as he wins. Brett won't be limited. He likes opportunities for advancement, having things set, and finishing the next step on the list. He studies engineering because he likes high-tech gadgets, it pays after graduation, and it's part of an elite world. Brett is also training to be a military officer. He likes marching and pageants; he keeps his shoes shined, his uniform straight, and his hair combed. But those who know him personally see a softer, humorous, playful side. He believes you have to have fun but also know when it's time to be serious about work. A good mix is important or people go crazy, he says, and he often relaxes with silly activities like watching cartoons. Naturally, Brett has lots of girlfriends.

Theme is planning and monitoring, ensuring predictable quality. Thorough, systematic, and careful. See discrepancies, omissions and pitfalls. Talents lie in administrating and regulating. Dependable, realistic, and sensible. Want to conserve the resources of the organization, group, family, or culture and persevere toward that goal. Thrive on planning ahead and being prepared. Like helping others through their roles as parent, supervisor, teammate, and community volunteer.

Other types to look at: ESTJ, ISFJ, ISTP

Planner Inspector
Temperament: Guardian
Interaction Style: Chart the Course
Cognitive Processes: S_i T_e F_i N_e S_e T_i F_e N_i

Stan (Corporate Manager)

Serious but good-natured, Stan is accustomed to managing and taking responsibility. He is a family man and loyal to the company that paid his way through college and has been his only employer. He makes tasks go as smoothly as possible and has difficulty understanding why some people are so disorganized or competitive, why they don't just do their jobs. Despite Stan's innate conservatism, he can be one of the boys when he's supposed to. He learned to fit in while training for football in high school and college; he also remembers dropping a girlfriend or two along the way because they were holding him back from jobs he really wanted. Stan strongly believes in community service. He helps coach high school football in the fall and does income tax as a side job in the spring. He camps, hikes, and fishes in his free time and teaches remedial life skills at a home for runaway youth. He enjoys helping other people's families, and his mother always wanted him to go into politics. Historical novels and a boyhood stamp collection are two hobbies he hasn't had much time for lately - Stan's company recently asked him to run several office training workshops for other managers, which means more office work. He and his wife have started going to the movies a lot in the past few years - stress-relieving escapism. Stan can also be quite a talker if you get him on a role, and he can get very enthusiastic about solid new projects, but in general he is contained.

Nina (Science Teacher)

Neat in appearance, sensitive and genteel but not bashful, open and receptive in conversation but deliberate and not overly talkative, Nina is generally very private and quite busy—a real problem solver. She's a retired army major, high school science teacher, and part-time inventor. Nina grew up in a poor neighborhood, returned to teach in the same area, and builds a lot of the school's equipment since it is often too expensive to buy. With a project, she needs paper and pencils when thinking, the object she's working on, and the necessary tools. Then she concentrates on a sample piece of the equipment in front of her or recollects in detail how a device with related features works. It's trial and failure. Nina's shop is laid out very orderly, very systematically, and she maintains her own tools. She can work for long stretches on the same problem with no need for breaks and dislikes interruptions. For relaxation, Nina enjoys sitting back and reading historical or theoretical books in her area. Her family does not always appreciate her working, but she strives to make time for them, doing family activities, and she really is quite motherly. Staying busy is comfortable. She sets her own standards to live up to, strives to do good work, and is proud of her inventions. Nina has written a short book on her admiration of the order in science. She instructs her students that education is important to lay the foundation but understanding comes from experience "out there." She's always talking about her time in the military and what she was told the first day of basic training: "The purpose is to survive."

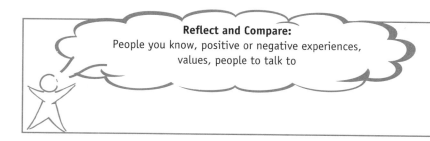

Reflect and Compare:
People you know, positive or negative experiences,
values, people to talk to

Norma (Beautician)

Norma is practical in all affairs, sensible and dependable. Her family and coworkers know her word is her bond. Her home is orderly and she runs a tight ship at the office, maintaining everything so people can do their work in peace. She makes sure her charges are properly trained, and without her accounting skills, the owner would have bankrupted their beauty salon years ago. Norma takes pride in that. And it's been hard to retire. She enjoys sports, ordering supplies and cleaning up, and driving the kids' teams around; she remembers the past and how important having an adult perspective was to her. She also loves the tranquility of the seaside. She's waiting for her husband to retire before moving her business to the ocean town they've picked out for their retirement, and in her experience, it should take about four years to develop a new solid clientele. She's planned for it. Her husband wants more of her time, but Norma would have no idea what to do with herself as a stay-at-home. It took six years to decide on marriage: she hadn't been sure if she could depend on one man for the rest of her life or if she really loved him, but eventually she took her grandmother's advice. And her grandmother wanted her to marry before she passed on. Norma's been very happy, although sometimes her husband's family's problems are a burden. She's accepted that you can't please everyone and she also backs him up. As she sees it, things are either right or wrong, and some people never learn.

Joe (Olympic Coach)

Players, fans, critics and bigwigs all know Coach. His sports manual on the art of "the game" and the psychology of success says it all. Joe is observant, intelligent and confident - these are all qualities he possesses and cultivates. He also enjoys making money and doesn't like to waste time or money on trivial things. He feels some people are too strict and rigid, and he remembers to enjoy parts of life other than making money. He reminds his athletes, "Take things in stride; don't let yourself get extremely frustrated or always push." That's one reason he's been elevated to serving on international sports commissions. The job requires a conservative diplomacy, getting committees formed to address everyone's concerns. Joe draws up planning manuals and develops uniform test methods, pass-fail criteria, and safety guidelines and standards - it's all part of shepherding any long-term program. And specifics require constant attention and additions to handle the unexpected. He tells people, "You may think this job doesn't prepare you, but it does." Hindsight is always twenty-twenty, and sometimes when he looks back, he realizes twenty years after the fact that he had other possibilities. But he keeps looking to new and more challenging goals. In the end, coaching is just doing what he does best. Joe enjoys leading people to better lives and likes some opposition to his ideas because when he implements an idea, he can be proud that he overcame adversity, resisted life's earthquakes. He reminds his athletes, "It's a hard world out there." What they see is just the tip of the iceberg.

Theme is providing, ensuring that physical needs are met. Talents lie in supporting others and supplying them with what they need. Genuinely concerned about the welfare of others, making sure they are comfortable and involved. Use their sociability to nurture established institutions. Warm, considerate, thoughtful, friendly. Want to please and maintain harmonious relationships. Thrive on helping others and bringing people together.

Facilitator Caretaker

Temperament:
Guardian
Interaction Style:
Get Things Going
Cognitive Processes:
$F_e S_i N_e T_i F_i S_e N_i T_e$

Other types to look at: ISFJ, ENFJ, ESFP

Mary (Businesswoman)

Mary is such a nice person! She's so pleased to meet new people and do fun activities. She gets a kick out of young people and really tries to help them along. She loves to be included and is very disappointed if she's left out, but she would never want to impose. She loves all the people she's involved with and has known over the years, and enjoys how interesting and what "a pack of fun" they all are. Mary likes to write. Her friends kept reminding her how many stories she had about the past and that maybe she should collect them into a book. Back in college on the swim team, Mary loved winning and was interested in going into business for herself - people need to be successful and make money to have a comfortable and convenient life. Then she met her future husband at a sorority party and decided that she should start a family. She was a swim coach for many years. Now, however, Mary has become a bit of an entrepreneur. She started with handicraft dolls and running for the local school board; and creating that cookbook was a real joy - to pull together all those family recipes - and it was such a pleasure to test them all out and perfect them! Mary also started her own bed-and-breakfast at her husband's suggestion. Of course, their financial picture was rock solid, so any money they made would be an extra. Mary knows she has a tendency to ramble and sometimes her hints to guests and employees are too subtle, but she's done her best to fix tensions between people. Of course, it's important to advertise for the right kinds of people in the first place. That ensures that life stays pleasant. These days, Mary's grandchildren are her pride and joy. What a treat they are!

Fernando (Dentist)

Devoted, sympathetic, and a hard worker. Fernando's parents supported him through dental school, and even though the science was difficult he learned because he had to, and it helped that his family knew that he could do it. For a time he got into fairly complex procedures and, being a natural at advertising, attracted a winning clientele and made a comfortable home. Now, twenty-four years later, the pleasure of golfing has grabbed him and he has become really skilled at it. He genuinely admires the pros and would love to play himself but feels he should maintain a tie with dentistry until his retirement to ensure a stable income and a sense of continuity for his teenage son, who is just starting to grow out of his disciplinary problems and let his dad back into his life. He encourages his son to take an interest in golf to help build their relationship. Fernando's wife and both his parents passed away a few years ago, and his therapist has tried to help him through, but sometimes times are difficult for him. He has been very close to his wife's troubled family since then. He has an intense sense of right and wrong and knows that he should be tactful and actively supportive through their trials and tribulations before the worst happens to them. Thank goodness the women at the office have been like a second family. His receptionist has always been there for him and now they've started dating. She encourages him to let out his concerns about who's accountable for what and any abuses of trust in his relationships. He appreciates her concern and empathy and figures that his son needs a mother. Now that's hard!

Sandra (Stage Performer)

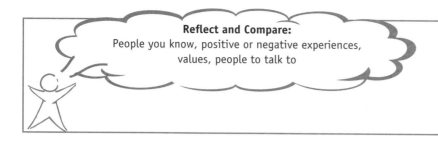

Sandra takes her music and her life, with all its fun, very seriously. That includes lyrics, album cover art, dance choreography, and the music. She's a singer in a group of gifted women who are practically family. They talk about men, relationships, and the issues they wake up to everyday. Sandra doesn't buy into the system and - when questioned - admits that the music is more than just about fun. It's about being heard and getting respect. People comment they feel they can be themselves around her. She speaks her mind, is very accepting of others, and has friends from all walks of life. She believes you shouldn't get bogged down in reasons why; you should hear people out, state how things are and help them face the issues. Sandra's been dating one guy several years now. She stands by him, supporting their political ambitions. Politics means community. She tries very hard and often feels it's her responsibility to work through the games and demand a standard of honesty and truth, whatever the problem. She often feels the real need to reconcile the past. That's what she brings to her lyrics, although most people only hear the issues: sticking hypocrisy back in people's faces. What she really loves is a show of romance: flowers, a serenade, a spontaneous kiss in the rain. Anniversaries are very important. Besides parties, friends, nights on the town, her work and her beliefs and heritage, it's these little things that really make life memorable and worth living.

Saul (Senator)

Politics is a fantastic challenging job—the greatest thing that ever happened to Saul—and he feels he could never totally retire. The community needs someone out there for them, and he loves to shake everyone's hand, hold babies, and be in front of the camera with his beautiful wife and young sons. He's taken a real interest in childhood development, brain research, education reform, and the importance of how we raise our children. There's a solution here. Saul looks out and sees a dog-eat-dog environment with how government is run these days—people hanging on and not being able to enjoy life and the country going down the tubes. Greed is a major concern, and people thinking they're above the law, not standing by their word. He would never just sit back in an office and then get on someone's case. He's a people manager. He says, "I want to help people work together as a team, and I just happen to be manager." He sits down so they feel a part of the team; then they talk over what they're going to do and how they're going to account for the cost of everything. At home, he's been teaching his children respect for their fellow people, and he's never had a problem with them. Saul would like more time together with his family, going places and sharing experiences. He and his dad have had a lot of good times together, and he wants to be there and not miss out as his own sons grow up. Saul and his best friend grew up as normal kids, and he loves sports and being out in nature - the change of seasons. Saul's life is good; he's very lucky. He can forget work when he comes home.

Theme is protecting and caretaking, making sure their charges are safe from harm. Talents lie in making sure everything is taken care of so others can succeed and accomplish their goals. Desiring to serve individual needs, often work long hours. Quietly friendly, respectful, unassuming. Thrive on serving quietly without fanfare. Devoted to doing whatever is necessary to ensure shelter and safety, warning about pitfalls and dangers and supporting along the way.

Other types to look at: ESFJ, ISTJ, INTP

Protector Supporter
Temperament: Guardian
Interaction Style: Behind the Scenes
Cognitive Processes: $S_i F_e T_i N_e S_e F_i T_e N_i$

Heather (Fashion Model)

Heather and her friends all agree that she is laid back and easy-going with a "whatever" attitude. She has been a model since the age of fourteen and has slowly been climbing her way into high fashion. She likes high-fashion because it is the best kind of work: you make the most money, travel the most, and receive a lot of perks. She especially likes shopping while traveling; naturally, she knows all she should about fashion and modeling, like the designer labels and how they rate. Stable, long-term relationships make Heather feel like she is doing okay and everything is set, and casually socializing with friends is a top priority. Right now Heather's career is still pretty secure and she is moving into acting. She did well in drama in school; acting seems routine for her and she hasn't had any preferences here. She definitely has artistic talent, and music and art have been hobbies since childhood. She hasn't forgotten how much her high school art teacher encouraged her. In any case, she has been careful to conserve her resources in life and use them wisely - she has saved up enough money to take nice vacations and sign up for classes at the local university to keep up with the business world and start preparing herself. Heather's sister recently got involved with a small but stable international company dealing with environmental products and is very happy there. But Heather says she would really prefer some kind of design work in the future, maybe fashion or interior decoration or even architecture. Whatever works out best will be fine with her.

Ken (Musician)

The life of a musician doesn't often provide as much as Ken would like but it's the band's sustained success, a sense of accomplishment, that keeps him in. The other guys know him as a quiet skilled musician and reliable and confidant with an insightful kind of common sense they often really need. Personally, he finds it really satisfying to listen to their problems and volunteer to help where he can, although the praise on stage once was really embarrassing. Mostly, Ken plays what he knows and what the band comes up with, remembering hundreds of tunes; he's not superimaginative and finds it a challenge to think of ideas and be creative—except in philosophy. Ken did great in that subject in college, and all those ideas have only become clearer and more important over time. He has a healthy respect for learning, and the different schools of thought and categories make philosophy easy to remember and use. Conversation doesn't usually reveal how really intelligent, well-informed and cultured Ken is, and he still enjoys the highbrow, aristocratic, classical music scene. His ponytail is his badge of honor as a member of the music culture, and he dislikes the annoying way society's institutions often invade people's private lives and make them feel bad. He really dislikes conflict—like when he drew the lot to fire the band's old manager—but he can face it because the other guys really watch out for him and because he feels he should treat them with the respect they deserve. Ken's usually in a long-term relationship, generally manages his own life well, and considers himself pretty idealistic. His hero is the adventurer Indiana Jones.

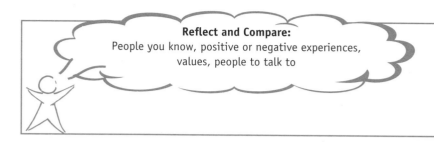

Reflect and Compare:
People you know, positive or negative experiences,
values, people to talk to

Tim (Police Officer)

Tim is really a good guy, reliable, and pretty funny. He wants people to feel at home around him, like the ritual Monday Night Football. Family is very important. Tim also likes to be where everything is happening. He likes riding around with his buddies in the squad car, just sitting back and observing. When walking the beat, he lets the kids know not to give him any lip or he'll have to take them down to the station. He tells people he's just doing his job as a cop, helping to protect the good citizens and make them safe from the few bad eggs. He understands that people certainly are entitled to feel the way they feel, but decisions have to be made and things have to go a certain way for everyone to live together, and the justice system gives people a chance to know what they did was wrong so they won't do it again. That's why he likes going into schools and talking, to paint the big picture for the kids before they're sucked in or get stuck in the middle of a bad situation. Sometimes it's a challenge for him not to overempathize when people tell him their stories, but he has to be tough to arrest them. It really bothers Tim to see those who are not pulling their weight because he feels he's a hard worker and is willing to get his hands dirty to get something done and do it in a quiet unselfish way. Tim's lived in the same area all his life. Security and familiarity are pretty important, and he really appreciates those people who reinforce those values, making it possible to work and live somewhere forever.

Carolyn (Technical Administrator)

Carolyn is a technical administrator. She coordinates programs nationwide for large companies that work with the handicapped. Organization - with a caring and detailed touch - is her strength. Her schooling as an engineer gave her the comfort with complexity and innovation that her job environment demands. With big projects she psyches herself up in advance, so that when the time comes, she's comfortable because she's pictured it in her mind. Being on the run with so many different things in her life, family and community and work, Carolyn does a lot of planning and coordinating with others in her head. When there's a problem, she does a lot of talking to people to get their ideas, then she gets to work quietly reconciling differences; she speaks to different groups individually so then she can put all the information together in a way that can satisfy everyone. Carolyn's own story is the hardship and dangers her family went through with her younger brother since his birth, and she's come to see over the years how important it is to share those kinds of experiences to make the connection and motivate people, to make them see that they're in good hands. She believes that people usually do the best they can with the resources they have, and Carolyn also grew up with the belief that people ought to be able to throw their cares into the fire at the end of the day and enjoy their accomplishments. Going home to family, especially her grandchildren, and gabbing with her few close friends - that's her reward. She's found that laughter and tolerance help people keep everything in perspective.

snapshot

Theme is directing and mobilizing. Talents lie in developing policy, establishing plans, coordinating and sequencing events, and implementing strategy. Excel at directing others in reaching the goals dictated by their strong vision of the organization. Thrive on marshaling forces to get plans into action. Natural organization builders and almost always find themselves taking charge in ineffective situations. They enjoy creating efficiently structured systems and setting priorities to achieve goals.

Other types to look at: INTJ, ESTJ, ESTP

Strategist Mobilizer

Temperament:
 Rational
Interaction Style:
 In Charge
Cognitive Processes:
 $T_e N_i S_e F_i T_i N_e S_i F_e$

Scott (Manager)

"Our Leader," Scott's colleagues call him. He's outgoing and a natural vision-ary, marshaling whatever it takes to make real progress happen. Scott is a manager at a software company where he schedules, structures, and optimizes people, time, ideas, and resources. He quickly purges inefficient policies and creates new ones that better serve long-range goals - every-thing must serve a logical purpose in the larger scheme of things. Consult-ing and hobbies fill his free time: rock-climbing, surfing, and networking with good people. They're all part of a self-improvement plan. When he was young, Scott got himself into a special school for gifted and talented students. He also grew up on the beach and got to know the surfers and beach people there. He is well aware of how easy it is for him to appear nerdy and get caught up in an elitist attitude, so he makes sure his friends outside of work are a diverse lot. Scott likes to invest in the stock market now and then and has been toying with the idea of finally starting his own company and being his own boss. So he works tirelessly while maintaining some balance. His vision is an Internet or other high-tech business - he knows he is really good at looking for solutions to fit the problems encountered in these areas, and he has also always been interested in educational reform and people's learning styles. On rare occasions, when he stopped to reflect on the past, he wrote one or two good short stories but he knows that being a professional writer requires a certain level of motivation and would be a lot to live up to.

Carla (Physical Therapist)

As a physiotherapist, Carla enjoys the time she spends intuitively exploring each patient, strategically putting in place systemic changes for them. Sometimes all that's required are a few probing questions, a few intelligent inferences, and a blunt reminder of the consequences of their current lifestyle. More often there is something seemingly impos-sible to work with - those who express understanding of what to do yet continue in their old patterns. She's learned to go slower to make the most of promising techniques, and whenever she sits down alone to map things out, the connections and relationships between the details just reveal themselves. She believes there is an art to this creative process—how the body locks in powerful thoughts and emotions—and she combines hypnotic suggestion, stories, and body work to weave a change, with the belief that with the correct application of the power of the mind and a strength of will, any miracle can be accomplished. Her patients describe her in paradoxical terms: intimidating, caring, wise, magical, overpowering, gentle, accepting, dismissive. "If only I could manage my time better," she shrugs. She has learned to enjoy tradition, and even at her age she loves working quietly in her cool garden to relax and be at one with the plants and her collection of reptiles - they fascinate her. And she still travels, to keep her mind curious and refreshed, always with an eye out for that promising young student who will be able to follow in her footsteps.

Analyze and Define:
Questions to identify or ask, qualities reflecting parts of yourself, changes to make, positive or negative experiences

Jean (Hospital Administrator)

Jean's thinking is systemic: the helm of even a small hospital requires comfort with complexity - rational policies and structures to ensure productive, efficient, democratic, and flexible processes. Except during her necessary ten-minute naps, Jean's door is always open. Everywhere her people shine, she takes advantage of, guiding and mentoring, knowing that each area is at different levels of readiness. Many people also see a lot of creative aspects to her personality. She has the ambition to venture into new areas and go through the creative process - knowing where to go next means researching the possibilities. She admires people with a lot of character and sees that in herself, staying focused and positive and pragmatic. She has a message to convey to people to make an impact on their lives. That's what medicine is about. And her thinking is futuristic: she's forged partnerships in new medical procedures and advanced technologies. Sometimes that means vigorous debate. Her philosophy is "solutions oriented." She's always thought that life is more than just about work. She knows what is important and what isn't and is not concerned about living in a philosophical world of moral questions and the task of self-improvement and evaluating one's beliefs. In moments of respite, with a cup of tea in hand, her life seems a far cry from that of the adolescent girl who informed her farmer parents that she would be going to college. Jean still goes back with her family to her parent's farm for vacations, where it all began, to maintain something very private.

Jared (Media Consultant)

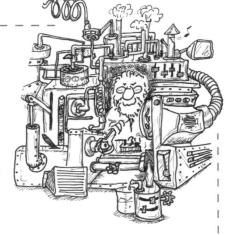

Jared has a dozen patents, is fluent in four languages, and is a poet and author of several major novels. Critics hail Jared among the premiere intellectuals of the day, and he has achieved success wherever he has applied his intellect. He has also found that successful prophets are often foreigners in their own land. Where he really broke through was at the side of a prominent media magnate, who mentored his potential, helped him develop patience and prepared a seat for him among the influential. His early career in international finance has provided money and a position to meet interesting people and be creative and self-directed. Jared loves classical music, the theatre, opera, and great literature and art - the finer products of civilization - and makes his home there. He's been blessed with two fine, unforgettable wives. He's sat on presidential panels, networks across disciplines, and finds it relaxing working with educated and open-minded "free thinkers." People know Jared as a man who's not afraid to get his hands dirty and get down to business, a leader across different groups. He can push his mind and body for projects and finds his greatest reward in entrepreneurial ideas, directing cutting-edge approaches to new media. Naturally, his strategies are always longterm, and his dearest and most daring vision is the construction of a lunar or orbital hotel - "the perfect place to relax in my old age and get away from it all." It helps that he's well acquainted with the president of the world's largest construction company.

snapshot

Theme is strategizing, envisioning, and masterminding. Talents lie in defining goals, creating detailed plans, and outlining contingencies. Devise strategy, give structure, establish complex plans to reach distant goals dictated by a strong vision of what is needed in the long run. Thrive on putting theories to work and are open to any and all ideas that can be integrated into the complex systems they seek to understand. Drive themselves hard to master what is needed to make progress toward goals.

Other types to look at: ENTJ, INFJ, ISTP, INTP

Conceptualizer Director

Temperament:
Rational
Interaction Style:
Chart the Course
Cognitive Processes:
N_i T_e F_i S_e N_e T_i F_e S_i

Tom (Engineer)

Tom is observing, intelligent, and confident - internally preoccupied with his own thoughts but outwardly pleasant to others. He has many objectives in his life, is careful to maximize opportunities to achieve them, and is accustomed to doing things alone because other people often detain him from getting things accomplished. Besides, his work style is intuitive flash first and then dressing it up with logic later. Tom enjoys his current job, but it is only a small part of his interests. He's trained as an engineer but he has many ongoing side projects and worldly experiences, including living in Africa for two years. Tom definitely needs time alone and spends hours scanning magazines, books, and shows about the latest scientific discoveries and trends. He takes the future very seriously, and a few ideas have stuck with him over the years. Nothing is too far-fetched if it can possibly be translated into reality. Tom actually enjoys people's company, and he notices a lot about people's true natures. Until recently, he rarely knew what to do with these insights. There are different parts of himself for different contexts, and he enjoys the feeling of self-improvement and learning how to enhance oneself. As in many areas of his life, Tom has turned his personal health and fitness into a science; he finds he must force himself to exercise but likes the results. Tom likes harmony and progress in his life and his relationships, and he requires freedom and time. He gladly shares his interests, ideas, and beliefs when another person brings up the topic and is capable of understanding.

Danielle (Psychology Student)

Danielle is a psychology student and local theater manager. She's always busy and has long felt it important to take advantage of the many unusual and exciting opportunities life can present. And there are a lot of directions to go. As a film buff, Danielle wrote a short script, bought a video camera, and has labored to make her movie just right, especially the visuals. Her friends keep mentioning it, but she has very serious - if unconventional - standards and tells them she'll get back to it and keep working at it until it's perfect. Danielle enjoys spending time with and meeting new people and has a large number of acquaintances, but only a few could be called "real" friends. She's easy to talk to but under pressure can be nervous and obnoxious. Danielle explains she thinks she should be doing more. She spends a lot of time socializing at the local coffee house, attending rock and Renaissance festivals, and surfing the Internet, and she likes extreme science fiction if it's good - she often says to herself she could write better. All these contribute to advancing who she is. Taking drama in school helped her a lot too, to outgrow herself, and her Audio-Visual club technical expertise helps her as a singer and with her guitar-playing. She's decided that working with troubled teens is more important than making money. Most people perceive Danielle - with her trademark counter-cultural hats - as a thoughtful person and often ask for her objective advice. Privately, she has always known what she wants to do with her life and how to accomplish that, even though her goal has changed a few times.

Analyze and Define:
Questions to identify or ask, qualities reflecting parts of yourself, changes to make, positive or negative experiences

Amanda (Astronomer)

All of Amanda's life has been about conceptualizing and working toward an abstract but powerful vision of the future that is hard to articulate. Her public career began after her first popular science book was hailed as a foretelling vision of things to come. In her mind, her work is about progress: humanity's place in the universe, the urgency for space exploration in a closed world, and the construction of a more rational, objective, and free society. She realizes that all this is a long way off. Years ago, Amanda broke into astronomy, and she has devoted a lot of her time encouraging girls in math and science. Involvement with government projects has been frustrating: funding for cutting-edge science versus a venue to the public. She dislikes trendy popular research like artificial intelligence - the present is already past, she says - and tries to maximize her time in promising esoteric areas like bio-electric energy. She involves her own children here. Amanda married late: marriage is the most important decision in one's life, and she thought deeply about what kind of man she should marry and the consequences of marriage on her work. Likewise, friends and colleagues are those who share and support her vision - others are discarded. It is the future that motivates and guides her, not some past; the reality is that understanding where people come from does not mean agreement because even when people agree they go on doing things differently. People tell Amanda she's in the prime of her life. She herself is sometimes haunted by the feeling of being born too early and caught in a time warp.

Paul (Private Investigator)

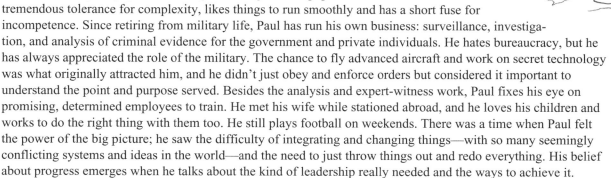

Paul is a strong individual, good family man and thoughtful community leader. He grew up in an active, sports-oriented family. Flying model planes led to piloting, and then he succeeded in his goal of making the Air Force academy. Paul's very knowledgeable, loves current events and thinking about what's really going on and what that will mean, and he can always be found reading the paper or working on his high-tech equipment. He has tremendous tolerance for complexity, likes things to run smoothly and has a short fuse for incompetence. Since retiring from military life, Paul has run his own business: surveillance, investigation, and analysis of criminal evidence for the government and private individuals. He hates bureaucracy, but he has always appreciated the role of the military. The chance to fly advanced aircraft and work on secret technology was what originally attracted him, and he didn't just obey and enforce orders but considered it important to understand the point and purpose served. Besides the analysis and expert-witness work, Paul fixes his eye on promising, determined employees to train. He met his wife while stationed abroad, and he loves his children and works to do the right thing with them too. He still plays football on weekends. There was a time when Paul felt the power of the big picture; he saw the difficulty of integrating and changing things—with so many seemingly conflicting systems and ideas in the world—and the need to just throw things out and redo everything. His belief about progress emerges when he talks about the kind of leadership really needed and the ways to achieve it.

snapshot

Theme is inventing. Find ingenious solutions to people and technical problems. Talents lie in developing ideas into functional and innovative applications that are the first of their kind. Thrive on finding new ways to use theories to make systems more efficient and people better off. Hunger for new projects. Have faith in their ability to instantly come up with new approaches that will work. Engineers of human relationships and systems as well as in the more scientific and technological domains.

Other types to look at: INTP, ENFP, ESTP

Explorer Inventor
Temperament:
Rational
Interaction Style:
Get Things Going
Cognitive Processes:
N_e T_i F_e S_i N_i T_e F_i S_e

Jake (Technical Consultant)

Ambitious and a bit cocky, Jake wants to find some interesting people with interesting ideas. He has lots of unbridled energy and at least a million questions and ideas running through his head, but he rarely finds someone to listen to all of them. Jake loves traveling and exploring new cultures and customs. He loves books on all topics, especially biographies and history, but has no time to read. He loves hi-tech gadgets. He has written magazine articles and imagines someday writing a great novel and making a lot of money. Jake is good at almost everything he applies himself to, and he gets bored with limiting jobs and dealing with all the details after thinking of an inventive idea. He gets bursts of motivation to work out to keep trim and energized, and his most creative ideas come then. He sees some of his ideas have been a little too creative, but at least he's passionate about them. He loves relationships and meets all kinds of people of all ages with ease; he has gone through seemingly millions of girlfriends and has almost married three times. He often wonders if he's ever going to meet the right person. Jake mainly works as a temporary in scientific jobs and early on rose to doing managerial work. He wins over people with a friendly demeanor, his playful humor, and his ability to catch people's true reactions in situations. Jake is always ready to learn from people if he really believes they know what they're talking about. His favorite job was as a travel agent and tour guide overseas, and he visited almost everywhere to write a book about life abroad. He found that was the most interesting lifestyle.

Janet (Motivational Speaker)

Janet's philosophy is an infinite world without limits. As an engineer in sales and marketing for twenty years in an unforgiving and relentless industry, she challenged herself to solve the technical problems of countless projects. And then she discovered the joy of books and the life of the mind. She still apologizes to old friends for being clueless about these things. It was her second husband and stress that made her realize that life is what we picture in our heads and that if she could build a formula that worked - constructing a picture for herself - a formula with purpose and a life of service in some way, then she could live her dreams and recapture her passion and inventiveness. The importance of family and relationships has kept Janet in close contact with those she loves; her children supported her the most in opening her health food store and returning to school to become some kind of therapist. At first she pictured psychiatry, but her unconventional interests and her gregarious personality drew her to a more stimulating life as a motivational speaker. Now she travels around the country and abroad several times a year, and in her workshops and television spots she shows literally millions of people how to become more successful. Janet tells her audiences that people sense when you are sincere and if you live your principles and are passionate then people will feel that about you. She believes that if people learn "the technology" and can imagine something, then materializing it really often is just one or two steps away.

Analyze and Define:
Questions to identify or ask, qualities reflecting parts of yourself, changes to make, positive or negative experiences

Andrea (Game Designer)

Andrea graduated early from high school and moved out on her own to take advantage of all the possibilities in life. At nineteen, she's the youngest regional manager for a nationwide computer gaming company. She works from home, a nice apartment she shares with friends. Virtual reality and interactive fiction are the hot topics, and she has a lot of fun while challenging herself to solve the problems she gets. Besides managing, she's directly involved in product development. Stories where you encounter mysteries, search for clues, and interact with others in a fictional world - they're her first love.

She prefers crime, detective and comic book themes, with a special interest in how people recover from bad situations in life. She formulates stories in terms of relationships and all the different possible plots to fix things. Each character gets a past history, pet peeves, and problems that motivate them. She plans the drama in terms of how each story line will turn out. Andrea also handles quite a bit of the computer artwork herself, both people and backgrounds. She did set design for school plays and uses lighting and other techniques to enhance realism. Andrea's friends are very important, and they talk a lot about what's going on in their lives. When people come over she makes them feel right at home, and she cares for and often thinks about others before herself. She fits in easily with adults and adult conversation and enjoys a weekly poker night. Her poker buddies are nice guys, idealistic and concerned about contributing to the future.

Eric (Political Advocate)

The public, his colleagues, and closest friends and family all know Eric in the same way. Character, common courtesy, and consistent principles are important to him. Eric's job right now focuses on advocacy for the public. It demands a lot of creative solutions, debate, fund-raising and a complex understanding of legislation. Part of the fun for him, as a lawyer in public service, is sparking stories that embarrass public officials. Eric grew up poor and feels this background led to what he does now. He read a lot as a child and could talk all day with interesting people - there's so much to learn - and he often wishes he could return to school and teach about philosophy and the mind. Science captures his imagination, he paints, and music is his first love - he switches between jazz piano, classical guitar, and bass. His dad has been a constant big influence, and he admires and thinks a lot about the intelligent, progressive people in his life. Eric has found it's really important that the people he's with match his level and intelligence. He feels bad when problems develop, and with his wife he's found talking without focusing on pure problem solving is important to working things out. This is also true at work, where he often has to make impromptu decisions for others' welfare, and he draws on his own experiences and the things that got him concerned and involved. Generally, he has very good diplomatic skills: very few leave with a bad impression and he shakes their hand even if they don't like him. Eric pictures himself being president.

Theme is designing and configuring. Talents lie in grasping the underlying principles of something and defining its essential qualities. Seek to define precisely and bring coherence to systems based on the pattern of organization that is naturally there. Easily notice inconsistencies. Enjoy elegant theories and models for their own sake and for use in solving technical and human problems. Interested in theorizing, analyzing, and learning. Thrive on exploring, understanding, and explaining how the world works.

Other types to look at: ENTP, ISTP, INFP, INTJ

Designer Theorizer
Temperament: Rational
Interaction Style: Behind the Scenes
Cognitive Processes: T_i N_e S_i F_e T_e N_i S_e F_i

Cameron (Computer Engineer)

Cameron prefers to work analytically amid the mountains of papers in his office as opposed to the chemicals and procedures in a lab. What he likes about his job is minimal supervision, no one looking over his shoulder. He likes the freedom to think clearly for himself and work alone without being hounded for practical applications. However, he can really get into the challenge of working with people: viewed from one perspective, it is a process of discovery. He enjoys, as he says, the intuitive experience, of just intuiting the right answer to a complex problem. Some insights are impressions; others are quite interesting and call for years of exploring, experimenting, and generalizing to make something crystal clear. Cameron lives this approach: be adaptable, accomplished, and competent. And he needs to be active - a day missed at the gym or without the beat of his trumpet leaves him feeling out of sorts, like he's losing his mind. With activities, a goal's really important—like biking all night to the top of a mountain and back. At work, he often scouts out innovative specialized equipment. The right restaurant, the choice vacation spot, the well-fitted suit - those make life enjoyable. When probed, Cameron likens himself to a computer: lots of peripherals, intertwined connections, and a central processor prioritizing a web of interacting programs and systems. Examining the nature of existence reminds him he enjoys learning more than working and is not always certain what to do. He enjoys investing and moonlighting as a community college instructor. His coworkers know him as friendly yet shy.

Linda (Psychologist)

Linda is a human-factors engineer. Generally seen as detached and calm, she works behind the scenes for the public and other engineers and psychologists in designing elegant machines that are easy to use. Linda doesn't deal with all the details of individual products. Her methodology is abstract and has been highly refined over three decades of focused work. Linda is considered an expert. She has published both a textbook and a popular book on her ideas. She also gives lectures and runs workshops for the public, for people in the industry, and for professors and college students at universities around the country. Her vision is of a future where inelegant boundaries between people and machines have been accurately figured out. Building connections with colleagues and working as part of a loose, informal team comes naturally, and she is often juggling many ideas and projects in her head at once. She has often ended up in demanding managerial positions, a role that comes only with effort. Linda and her husband have been together since high school, and she relies on him to organize their social events and home life. Her friends are her colleagues, and many of her employees are her children and their families. She likes the idea of connecting socially but finds her work devours any free time. Linda, and everyone who knows her, can say that with all her interests she will never get bored, with or without an office, work, or job. Working from a theoretical people focus, she strategically nurtures her own personal development.

Analyze and Define:
Questions to identify or ask, qualities reflecting parts of yourself, changes to make, positive or negative experiences

Anna (Screenwriter)

There are no typical days. As a screenwriter and actress, Anna's often subject to bouts of inspiration, and outside input (a book, an afternoon at the museum) helps activate her imagination - she gets struck by a theme that she wants to explore. It's often hard to communicate. Artistic merit means something well-crafted and true to a certain perspective. She likes a hero who is the analytical guy in the corner, the one you would never suspect. In acting, Anna can be someone else. It's a fantasy, momentarily living a different life. Some lines make her heart sing, and she takes pleasure in exploring what seems magical, like a device people could use to transmit images from mind to mind. And each idea sparks many more pictures in her head until the pieces crystallize, taking on a certain arrangement or form. Film is art, and art is abstract communication. Things like magazines, picture books, talk radio, film, and a few intelligent, serious TV shows - she watches the process of interaction, and the themes to develop are the interesting ones others should know. When Anna gets an idea, she can't think about anything else until she does something with it; it's very exciting and then there's the "creative hangover." When pitching an idea to a studio, she finds it's often hard to encapsulate it in words, but at least she's there to answer questions as they come up. It takes a lot of introspection, the clarity to differentiate between what she refers to as "reality" and the "real reality." Anna knows all too well that she's atypical.

Marcus (Music Professor)

As a child prodigy, Marcus was performing at age four, conducting at fourteen, and working as a university music professor before twenty. The mathematical beauty behind the music excites him. Marcus is very political. His ivory-tower life strikes him as less tangible than the human rights issues out in the real world. He has a strong if vague sense of how the powers that be move people away from the fundamentals of human nature, as well as a strong sense of individualism and the importance of dignity and independent thought. His passion is crossing the artificial borders and arbitrary laws that divide and confuse, and he takes music to different corners of the world. Demonstrations and protests over the claptrap of pop textbooks often land him in hot water. His brightest students, the innovative thinkers who clearly grasp the theory, have a special place in his heart. Marcus is good at juggling the many aspects of music at once. He's very aware when things don't flow and cannot tolerate imprecision. He has few equals who hold themselves to the same level of competence, who are able to detach themselves from the music, and he spends hours, sometimes days, in deep concentration. The passage of time is often a problem, and he finds respite at a cabin in the woods, living a simple life free of social demands and technological distraction of the mind. For companionship, he longs for perfection somewhere out there that he just hasn't met yet. If only he could keep track of his clothes and when to eat—having those things just taken care of would be music to his ears.

Theme is mentoring. Lead people to achieve their potential and become more of who they are. Talents lie in empathizing with profound interpersonal insight and in influencing others to learn, grow, and develop. Lead using their exceptional communication skills, enthusiasm, and warmth to gain cooperation toward meeting the ideals they hold for the individual or the organization. Catalysts who draw out the best in others. Thrive on empathic connections. Frequently called on to help others with personal problems.

Other types to look at: INFJ, ESFJ, ESTP, ESFP

Envisioner Mentor

Temperament:
Idealist
Interaction Style:
In Charge
Cognitive Processes:
F_e N_i S_e T_i F_i N_e S_i T_e

Diana (Company Liaison)

Diana is warm and friendly, with a sincere smile that warms the heart and an intensity that lets people know there is more to her than meets the eye. Diana just got her degrees in biology and English literature, and a summer internship her senior year turned into the job she has now. The people around her are not surprised at how quickly she has risen through the ranks: she has a keen knack for knowing people and what is important to them, works hard to make others' lives run smoothly, and offers emotional strokes to make people feel good and heal relationships. She feels intelligent and needed at her job, but she gets the feeling she intimidates some of her male coworkers. Dating is very important. She has fashioned her own style and loves to go out and feel desirable, and her goal is a secure career and successful family with a man who will shower her with love, respect, and attention. Diana knows her life is now in transition; she's very interested in how her life will turn out and looks for ways to figure out where she's headed. She knows she's eventually returning to school in preparation for her future as some kind of facilitator, healer, or human relations consultant. She admires people for who they are and knows what they need, but she also feels people need to experience and learn for themselves the same realizations in life she's had. That's what she savors from her favorite existential writers—the words that move mountains. Diana also plays classical piano masterfully and foresees this will always be part of her life. It means so much.

Gideon (Playwright)

Playwright, musician, diplomat, pillar of neglected communities—whatever outlet he chooses for his intuitive inspirations—Gideon explains to critics and fans, he is expressing his feelings and communicating his perceptions so he can be a part of their lives. Family, friends, community, earth—there are lessons to be learned and everyone needs to grow. He channels his desires for others creatively. He paints and sketches and designed his own home. With his plays, Gideon really enjoys the process of connecting with characters and weaving the moral of the story, showing how people can make their relationships successful and grow to understand how the universe works through knowledge and its wise application. Tell him a new insight into human behavior or how things relate, and Gideon is there, curious and encouraging, helping to plant the seeds of realization and new levels of awareness. Life is not just about creating ideas but what happens to them. Then there are the "endarkened" - the hurtful, selfish and frightening. Sometimes it feels like people sit and expect him to work miracles - he reminds them that they choose their own life path. There are also times of truce, introspection, reconciliation, and being in love - ordinary people in extraordinary circumstances. Gideon often speaks of the joy of relinquishing the need to change people by living in the present; he envisions a world at peace, united through the healing power of compassion and diplomacy. Political speech writer, translator of foreign works, self-help guru of sorts - he also appreciates and enjoys a fine international lifestyle of money and security.

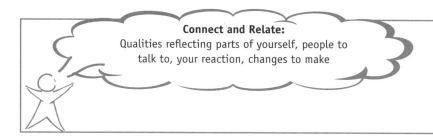

Connect and Relate:
Qualities reflecting parts of yourself, people to talk to, your reaction, changes to make

Jerome (Technical Writer)

Jerome is "Mr. Mom." He goes to school, raises the kids, and works part-time from home - writing technical documentation for computer users, including diagrams. Making computers user friendly is very important, and he displays his polished, published work. The home is a full-time job. His wife is a lawyer and they enjoy entertaining. He supported her through school and now she supports him - like chefs or gardeners cooperating to create something together or trusted traveling companions on a shared journey. Their three children are a joyous handful: soccer and hockey, piano and violin lessons, the swim team and school plays. Watching them mature into who they are as individuals is important and exciting. He's so proud and tells them so. Jerome is a Boy Scout leader and started a PTA panel: "Ethics in the Classroom." He swims - exercise helps him work out problems. He's not as technical as some incredible students in his computer classes, but learning became easier after he awoke one morning to realize that programming is a "design" problem. It's like his hobby, drawing house floor plans and building and remodeling. (He dreamed as a kid he would become "some kind of architect.") Now he understands programming and has the highest grades. The military was Jerome's ticket to his security now. It helped pay his way to his degree and provided life skills. He values the military for the same reason he values the scouts - it helps people improve themselves with honor and respect, teaches "facts before assumptions," and encourages people to work together to overcome obstacles.

Lorena (Communalist)

Lorena is earthy, dedicated, and other-worldly, a mother for the entire community. She is at the center of a summertime farm commune where people come to share their worldly goods as well as their insights and life journeys. She enjoys the outdoors, the animals and simple comfortable living. Lorena supervises the teaching of the children, planning what needs to happen. This is her most important role. If she's going to make an impact, then she must reach them early, with a keen and authentic insight into each child as an individual. Children need lots of love and nurturing, and she always praises them and makes them feel good when she comes into the schoolhouse. She takes over personally when it comes to their personal development, how to tune into and feel okay about their intuitive experiences. They talk about the future of the world, sharing stories of their parents' dedication and sacrifice - not letting anyone squelch or sabotage their dreams or who they are, not being afraid. It's what she wished she'd had as a child. Lorena also works on creative projects that emerged from the otherwise alienating cluelessness she experienced in medical school, and she and her husband have forged an intense and loyal bond and look forward to having their own children soon. Lorena also acts as commune sibyl, interpreting symbolic events. She often hopes the people will grow faster with just a little more facilitation, to fight their resistance and open their eyes. Sometimes she can just "see" into people and hear them calling out for help, and she accepts the onus of manifesting the vision and potential.

Foreseer Developer

Temperament:
Idealist
Interaction Style:
Chart the Course
Cognitive Processes:
$N_i F_e T_i S_e N_e F_i T_e S_i$

snapshot

Theme is foresight. Use their insights to deal with complexity in issues and people, often with a strong sense of "knowing" before others know themselves. Talents lie in developing and guiding people. Trust their inspirations and visions, using them to help others. Thrive on helping others resolve deep personal and ethical dilemmas. Private and complex, they bring a quiet enthusiasm and industry to projects that are part of their vision.

Other types to look at: ENFJ, INTJ, INFP

Julia (Political Activist)

Julia's idealism has driven her against all odds. Her private life themes and vision of a world at peace has carried her from the solitude of the studio, to volunteering with runaway teens off the street to the publicity of the occasional government podium. Even as a young girl, Julia found herself sensitively attuned to the unique gifts and personal destinies of the desperate people around her, and she has often channeled these impressions into her artwork, trusting the magic in her intuitive gifts above all else in connecting with the sometimes hostile individuals who've arrived on her doorstep. It's so important, she says, to feel things out and discover commonalties before self-disclosing. For Julia, the environment is also a guiding cause, and anticipating what she can afford to care about is important. The weight of relationships and her art has often drained her, and even as a healthcare consultant herself, illness has struck when the stress of conflict has been greatest. And she's found that time in complete isolation with her art - the freedom to be sentimental and romantic - will act as a powerful cathartic release, especially when she allows images and feelings of the fantastic and wild to emerge over the fine techniques and texturing she usually attends to. That's the covert power of the psyche. Julia also loves to travel. Ironically, it has been the widespread poverty, persecution, and hatred she's witnessed - balanced by her husband's unconditional support - that have sustained her vision of a world united by more humane and just sensibilities.

Justin (Actor)

The science fiction action heroes Justin has portrayed on film are not quite the sensitive, insightful guy his friends and family know. Justin views the art of acting as illusion, portraying the untrue. He likes the idea of strangers knowing who he is without really knowing him. Action without risk, being the man for every women—that's what's appealing. He's also enjoyed atypical serious roles but avoids anything forcing a message. Justin loves politics - observing people play out their personal issues before the world - and he's had fun being in the spotlight. The money's nice, the parties great, if transitory, and he likes exploring the singles world as a star. Dating has been somewhat of a strain, although if the woman can deal with the fame, then usually he's been okay too. He laughs at the tabloids, hasn't forgotten his longtime friends, and has often felt he has to make time to visit with everyone. Justin has a strong intuition for good parts. He has been able to tell what will do well, what's a good role, and what's commercially viable. He's really proud of some of his work, and has carefully used his name to get his fiction published. Writing has meant not neglecting his inner true self, but he tells people being a full-time professional writer would make him grow to dislike his gift. Justin owns a classy ski resort bar, a relaxing place where people can just get together and talk. And he likes feeling free on his motorcycle, though he's been a little accident prone, and he likes his computer - a space to engage his mind. He says, "The future and the mind—now that's powerful!"

Connect and Relate:
Qualities reflecting parts of yourself, people to
talk to, your reaction, changes to make

Adam (Graduate Student)

All through life, the people Adam has met have helped change how he thinks and his perspectives. Adam is a graduate student in college, where he's also a librarian. He returned to college after working for several years when he couldn't seem to find a meaningful niche. He's done well in his major, and the professors and other students really like him - he's friendly, sort of shy, and usually laid back unless he is under a lot of pressure - but he's unsure about what he's studying. He's good at a great many things: art and music, computers and architecture, film and creative writing, biology and photography. He pays attention to popular music and clothes, and it takes only a few minutes of conversation to reveal how intelligent and insightful he is. Adam's also very comfortable in relationships and bridging emotions; he and his previous girlfriend recently parted on good terms. They had been living in different cities and he flew out just to end the relationship smoothly and maintain their friendship. The meaning of relationships has been very important. Adam worked in radio in college and has kept up with his old music buddies; he wants to be there for those times when they come for help and advice. It pains him when the solution is right there and they haven't gotten it - then they need space to work things out on their own. There is almost a mystical quality to Adam, but he can also easily be deliberately obnoxious and evocative when he needs to - that's the appeal of radio - as a wake-up call on insincere behavior. To no one's surprise, Adam is considering walking across the country after he graduates.

Madeline (Software Developer)

Madeline enjoys the technical lab along with the human side of her business—training, education, and software—and she's dealt a lot with groups. Her own first group experience was a powerful awakening. With core issues, she calls things as she sees them and through a metaphor or analogy turns the situation into a growth opportunity - the joy of seeing things click and eyes open. It's all part of a cycle, and anchoring her creative insights into what gets results has also helped keep her going. For Madeline, it's about respect, equality, and illuminating what's offensive. The most fascinating situations have appeared completely normal on the surface, and she's very aware of group behavior, the stages groups pass through, and how people end up taking on roles. Her saying: "Intimacy means being in the here and now." Teaching is selling, selling is teaching, and she's usually been confident of what group participants can handle. Madeline just "knows" what their experience will be like. This is part of her lifelong task of explaining how she knows what she knows and the ethics of acting as a catalyst. Madeline's also terribly thankful with her luck on the stock market. She tends to make moves others call risky, but she goes in with her eyes open, ready to live with an outcome, and people remark on her comfort with emotions. Her life includes workshops, phone work, analysis, research and design, and daily yoga. Her kids and husband are also full-time careers, and she juggles, chauffeurs, and replans as needed. Sometimes she just has to laugh at the paradox in her day, at what it takes, as she says, "to rattle the cage."

Theme is inspiration, both of themselves and others. Talents lie in grasping profound significance, revealing truths, and motivating others. Very perceptive of others' hidden motives and purposes. Interested in everything about individuals and their stories as long as they are genuine. Contagious enthusiasm for "causes" that further good and develop latent potential and the same zeal for disclosing dishonesty and inauthenticity. Frequently moved to enthusiastically communicate their "message."

Other types to look at: INFP, ENTP, ESFP, ESTP

Discoverer Advocate
Temperament: Idealist
Interaction Style: Get Things Going
Cognitive Processes: $N_e\ F_i\ T_e\ S_i\ \ N_i\ F_e\ T_i\ S_e$

Carrie (Corporate Headhunter)

Carrie is exuberant, charismatic, and charming, with a subtle magical quality that compels others to follow her while drawing out their hidden potential. Her circle of friends and career ambitions keep her busy and happy - life is meaningless without people to relate to and boring without change. It's those "ah ha" perceptions that inspire her as an executive headhunter and organizational facilitator. It's a lot of aspects combined, and she's glad she has the knowledge she does because when the relationships are good, then everything flows. She hates even the word "limit." Hidden to most people, Carrie runs through a dozen moods a day - many levels of feeling, each changeable or constant in a different way. And she loves to stay up with someone half the night and become the best of friends in search of themselves - "This is who I am, I am this person." Outside of work and socializing, she enjoys reading, films, abstract art, and music. Although seemingly disorganized in juggling many things at once, Carrie is incredibly effective with people. She knows she has always been a natural counselor: eager to help, interested in what others believe, perceptive of the possibilities in others, an enthusiastic and genuine listener, and someone who wants to be at the center of things but not necessarily the topic of conversation. And friendliness aside, Carrie is blunt with phony people. What she really loves is to be surprised by learning something new and discussing new perceptions about someone she thought she knew. And sometimes she herself is that someone.

Peter (Writer-Director)

Peter, an up-and-coming writer-director, expresses surprise at the tremendous response to his work. He sees stories as case studies of the human condition and seeks to explore and convey the feeling of a theme in each work, especially love in all its curious and ironic forms. Peter lives the creative process—its productive spurts and dry spells—and in going into a meeting on new projects, it's his belief in the story, in others, and in himself that he weighs. His career demands much, assures little, and his perception is that life and love are what one makes of them. That's why he's inquisitive about the intriguing people he encounters and refuses to indulge their weaknesses; their lives inspire him with the courage to take his audience to the limit emotionally and then to upset those emotional assumptions. How pleasing it would be to see an insightful book in every school, one that actually connects. Ironically, he finds his young son the most bewildering person of all. Peter jets between his oceanfront beach house, his Las Vegas ranch, and life in the big city. He delights in good food, a game of chess, travel, sports, and women. Inconsistent though he may be with all of these, he still feels the nostalgic pull of an earlier life of action as a professional cyclist. His own story: he travels like a stranger in search of those rare, intelligent, and perceptive individuals who can recognize the truth and possibilities in the world. Running clears his head; the high transforms him into a well-oiled machine. He's often heard to remark how uncanny it all is.

Connect and Relate:
Qualities reflecting parts of yourself, people to
talk to, your reaction, changes to make

Phineas (Actor)

Phineas always finds himself at the center of everything interesting while
magically immune to lasting trouble. For a time he found both excitement and
discipline. Entranced by the life of a fighter pilot - a man in his machine,
flying alone through the clouds - Phineas entered the military at age seventeen
and soon found himself in front of a news camera. Journalism still piques his
interest, and he's sampled acting and modeling and massage school - so many
possibilities and ready to try anything but only one life to live. Whatever he
does, his buoyant flow of happiness lets people know it's okay to be who they
really are with him. He also finds that a more mellow mood is very comfortable
and productive, and travel often produces the change of pace he needs to settle himself
down. He meets total strangers with ease and has forged his closest friends in the unlikeliest
of circumstances. He's always there for his friends, is very loyal, and asks much of them. Everyone knows
Phineas has a loving heart and is always willing to make a more meaningful connection. He has an
awareness of people's energy and what to do with that, and his talent and affinity for martial arts acts as
a focus in life: it brings a lot into his awareness and has gotten him out of trouble on many occasions.
Sometimes Phineas reflects on how it is, living with himself, being an effortless natural at everything that
doesn't lead to a conventional life. Maybe he'll enter politics - "Just more acting," he says - and make
sweeping changes. He dreams of settling down on a farm with a white picket fence and the woman he
loves. Then he'd feel content.

Marina (Artist)

Abstract art is something Marina's good at and can be creative with - that sense of adventure and being totally
in the situation. She's very hands-on and perceived by others as energetic and strangely fascinating. Marina likes
the idea of living in a different time—of waking up one day and finding everything is completely different—or
meeting a long-lost twin. In art, she believes in creating something with unique appeal and loves the fact that
other people think she's weird. She combines photos and paintings. She never goes out and just randomly takes
pictures. Everything is set up professionally: clothes, props, backgrounds, lighting.
She wants recognition, and the commercial side is good: to be notorious in
turning people on to the deeper meaning. She enjoys her freedom to act on a
creative mood, to choose the medium to convey an inspiration - the constant
search for something truly original. Marina never ignores her values. Art has really
helped her along in life. Only a few people understand. Marina enjoys staying at
home, curled up on her couch and enjoying her creature comforts. She loves to
read; it's how the story is told that satisfies her. Silence is good. That's what she
likes about her artist boyfriend. They're together but in their own space, doing
their thing, separate but together, and that feels genuine. She loves to dress up -
clothes, makeup, and hair always put together. And she explores both the light
and the dark sides, in her art and her life, exposing the superficial. What counts
is treating each other like human beings.

snapshot

Theme is advocacy and integrity. Talents lie in helping people clarify issues, values, and identity. Support anything that allows the unfolding of the person. Encourage growth and development with quiet enthusiasm. Loyal advocates and champions, caring deeply about their causes and a few special people. Interested in contemplating life's mysteries, virtues, and vices in their search for wholeness. Thrive on healing conflicts, within and between, and taking people to the center of themselves.

Other types to look at: ENFP, ISFP, INTJ

Harmonizer Clarifier
Temperament:
Idealist
Interaction Style:
Behind the Scenes
Cognitive Processes:
F_i N_e S_i T_e F_e N_i S_e T_i

Patty (Psychologist)

Patty is deep and mysterious. She appears full of contradictions yet has a certain tranquility about her: she is serious but loves to have fun, she is warm and inviting but appears to have many layers she does not reveal, she is multi-talented but focused. Patty is trained as a psychotherapist but more recently has begun writing children's fantasy stories - she has always loved books and stories, especially humor, folklore, myth, and religion. Telling a good story at the right moment has always come naturally, and she's recently discovered the power of storytelling with clients. Patty keeps in touch with her network of eclectic friends and acquaintances, writing letters and sending quirky postcards. She also illustrates her own stories, something she has always been good at. And she listens to a lot of different kinds of music and reads voraciously. One of her favorite pastimes is spending an afternoon at the local university library. She takes a few books off the shelf, finds a comfortable and relaxing spot, and reads right there. Growing up, Patty did everything - after-school activities, honors classes, community service. Her family just assumed she would be an English teacher like her father, and she never envisioned otherwise - reading and writing have always helped her work out how she feels about her values. Then a truly wonderful college professor introduced her to psychology, and the experience inspired her to fulfill her beliefs and natural talents there. She approaches each client with an enthusiasm for sharing and respect for that person and where he or she is coming from.

Jim (Writer)

Genuine, witty, serious, a believer—Jim is a writer and his fictional alter ego "Jim" is an agent of the federal government, a field investigator in criminal cases. Sometimes something unusual or unexpected turns up, and it's those odd cases, the really mysterious or heinous ones, that become compelling causes within him. For these, solving the puzzle or capturing the suspect is always a triumph. His colleagues see the crusader in him; Jim feels the challenge of structure and planning required. People's rationales and perspectives emerge from their deepest beliefs, and he always enjoys putting ideas on the table for discussion, just as much to observe people as to explore the case at hand. And intuition plays as much a role as the evidence. Jim's alter ego also pursues a secret life as a writer, having published three novels over the years. For the real Jim, his work isn't any particular genre but what just might lie beyond the veil of everyday life. He finds writing subtly communicates what's important, and books stand out there as a guiding force. It's about believability. He never planned on this job or his life but can't imagine doing otherwise. Jim does have a reputation as being somewhat unorthodox, and his colleagues see that as a strength. He's naturally suspicious of government, and that makes him even happier "to be working on the inside, or from the inside," as he says. Jim can be very persuasive, adaptable, and cool under fire as publishing deadlines approach. He lives to uncover the truth. Sometimes the universal issues feel so big he doesn't know where to start.

Connect and Relate:
Qualities reflecting parts of yourself, people to
talk to, your reaction, changes to make

Ezra (Medical Doctor)

Self-purification begins at home. Ezra fondly remembers when, as a fresh, idealistic medical doctor, he signed on alone for a simple missionary life of quietly bringing reassuring comfort and enlightenment to the suffering and poor abroad. Decades later, his experiences of good and evil and his search for the meaning of his values led to a book collecting his insights into how people deal with the deepest moral and ethical issues that face all human beings—how the events in people's lives shape their emotions, the moral turning points, the choices and role of free will, the joy of becoming reacquainted with oneself. Ezra wanted something scientific and concrete, not just an abstract or philosophical work. He wanted to give some structure to it, so he wove all those true stories into a number of carefully thought-out "conceptual meditations on life." He feels it all comes down to freedom to live one's ideals and loyalty to those ideals. And he stresses accepting people as they are, action in the face of contradiction, and sensitivity to the struggle in the world balanced with a need to get on with one's day. The visceral, simple life still calls, but the spirit never rests. In times that he's felt he's lost his bearings and is tired and worn out, he rediscovers the need for genuine community, always ever-closer to home, and that revitalizes him. He hears quiet cries for help, and one day the people and resources just come together; then he finds himself floating once again into a leadership role. Like rocks in a stream, he says, we cannot apologize for all the truths left unsaid.

Allison (Comedian)

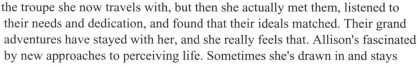

Allison is an enigma to all her suitors—very focused and professional yet spontaneous and drawn to extremes. Often it's her inner reaction to insights about her relationships that puts her in a state of questioning. Idealistic though it may be (and as she says at "work"), what comes around goes around in the universe and she will conduct herself properly. As a professional comedian, Allison believes in exploring everything, the whole marvelous and bizarre human experience. At first she didn't want to get involved at all with the troupe she now travels with, but then she actually met them, listened to their needs and dedication, and found that their ideals matched. Their grand adventures have stayed with her, and she really feels that. Allison's fascinated by new approaches to perceiving life. Sometimes she's drawn in and stays up all night; ideas gel and she discovers a whole new realm of delicious humor to explore. Political satire and horrid relationships are her favorite topics. She finds real humor is about listening to what's not said, letting people fill in the blanks for themselves as much as possible - she always has a strong sense of what an audience is ready and eager for. Sometimes she plops down on stage and just asks a person in the front row what's really going on, to laugh at themselves. It's all about that eternal pull: the romantic and charming animal or the wise and brave intellectual. She always looks to her sisters and longtime friends for support and finds her private poetry a release. Sometimes she's a real mystery even to herself.

Flavors of Type

Sixty-four varieties of people is a large net to cast in understanding yourself and others. And the four characters presented with each type hardly exhaust the true variety available to us. In the characters you identified with for yourself and others, what commonalities do you find? What differences? Explore the dimensions below.* Some will speak to you; others won't. Discover what

has shaped your life. Does your natural style, career, and personal life align or not? Can you live with any mismatches, or is change needed? What effect are your choices here having on others?

BEFORE YOU CONTINUE	
Take a moment to integrate what you've learned so far	
Your Temperament Pattern	
Your Current Life-Themes	
Your Best-Fit Type Pattern	
Biographies That Matched	

Participative or Independent Style?

Some people are clearly more introverted and solitary by nature, preferring to let other people initiate things, but they nonetheless participate with confidence out in the world with others, often as a member of a group. These people are more participative. Similarly, many people prefer extraverting and initiating relationships but also find themselves working quietly with insight and direction or out in the world but on their own. These people are more independent. Similarly, one may be an independent introvert or a participative extravert. If career choice does not match a person's natural style, or if a couple has styles that put them individually on the same path or in conflict with each other, then the flavor of the relationship will change. Two different styles can complement each other or not.

My Style	My Career Requires	My Personal Life Requires
☐ Participative Style ☐ Independent Style WHY?	☐ Participative Style ☐ Independent Style WHY?	☐ Participative Style ☐ Independent Style WHY?

Local or Global Perspective?

Some people are more grounded in immediate local concerns, while others find themselves on a larger stage with broader concerns. Career aspirations and the space we leave, large or small, in our lives to have close relationships often reflect our perspective. Two global people may find little to fall back on in support of each other. A mix means mutual support. The abstract temperaments (Rational and Idealist) can appear like the concrete temperaments (Guardian and Artisan) when they have a local perspective. Similarly, a Guardian or Artisan with a global perspective may appear to others like a Rational or Idealist. Thus the flavor!

My Perspective	My Career Requires	My Personal Life Requires
☐ Local Perspective ☐ Global Perspective WHY?	☐ Local Perspective ☐ Global Perspective WHY?	☐ Local Perspective ☐ Global Perspective WHY?

*For readers familiar with the MBTI, the four ways above of looking at the flavors of the sixteen types is not meant to stand for or be a replacement for the four-letter MBTI code. These flavors are variations on personality that help explain important differences between people of the same type.

Softer or Harder Demeanor?

Anyone of any temperament or type may present a tougher or softer exterior to the world. A harder side often meets success-oriented needs. A softer side often develops out of the process of self-change and self-awareness. A hard edge can grow soft, and a soft edge can sharpen with age and experience. Relationships can have a powerful effect. Friends, couples, and relatives often grow to be more alike. Sometimes it may seem like nice guys finish last and the determinism of the harder approach is rewarded—but at what cost? Work and home are inseparable, and paradoxically, a softer demeanor–fewer walls and boundaries–also keeps us open to creative input, work relationships, and insights that ultimately make success possible.

My Demeanor	My Career Requires	My Personal Life Requires
☐ Softer Demeanor ☐ Harder Demeanor **WHY?**	☐ Softer Demeanor ☐ Harder Demeanor **WHY?**	☐ Softer Demeanor ☐ Harder Demeanor **WHY?**

Mainstream or Counter-Cultural Attitude?

Not all Guardians are conventional. Similarly, others may wear a conventional hat or a counter-cultural one, varying with whether or not their needs and values are being met by mainstream society. Differences between people here often hide deeper attitudes and issues. In most cases, society provides a basic track for people to follow to success–slow and steady but with little risk and far less chance of innovation or great reward. Conversely, when we move off this track we can go our own way at our own pace, but the risks are greater and there is usually only a small safety net. Our culture's model expects a plan from us as soon as possible, which is often impossible. But too much counter-culture will eliminate possibilities.

My Attitude	My Career Requires	My Personal Life Requires
☐ Mainstream Attitude ☐ Counter-Cultural Attitude **WHY?**	☐ Mainstream Attitude ☐ Counter-Cultural Attitude **WHY?**	☐ Mainstream Attitude ☐ Counter-Cultural Attitude **WHY?**

Now that you have seen some of the mechanisms behind the different flavors of type, it may be clearer why you related to some character sketches and not others–each flavor of each of the sixteen types answers each of the four dimensions above in a different way. Within your *best-fit type*, you may have resonated with one, two, or possibly three characters while rejecting the rest. With different types, you probably found some characters who felt foreign while one or two outside your *best-fit type* may have felt friendly and welcoming. We may resonate with someone of another type because their flavor is the same as ours. The flavors explain the commonalties and differences that unite and divide us regardless of temperament and type.

Remember that each life-theme encourages its own culture. Visit a new life-theme–you will encounter people who reflect attitudes and beliefs different from your own, and you will discover not just something new to grow but a new way to grow. We are called to learn to stretch to the other side. How we respond reflects our character.

> ▼ **C H A R A C T E R** ▼
>
> Character results from what the world gives you and how you choose to act and respond.

Tests of Character

Everyday we're tested with challenges and opportunities we have to act on and respond to. How we act and respond is influenced by our temperament needs and values and our type theme.

We've seen character as temperament needs, values and talents; character as life-themes that give meaning; and character as a unique personal history that sets us apart. There is a fourth meaning.

> ▼ C H A R A C T E R ▼
>
> Character as morals and ethics: Taking responsibility for how we respond, for ourselves and others, to the consequences of our actions–or inaction–intended or not, particularly in our careers and relationships.

Two Moral Visions

Although temperament, type and other frameworks presented here seem to suggest that values are relative, there is in fact an unequivocal moral and ethical imperative behind the work of those who originated and sustain these ideas, and who perceive a genuine connection between character and personality. In particular, the moral visions of Isabel Myers and David Keirsey are responses to our everyday need for character.

Study of the sixteen types, while based on the ideas of Carl Jung, began in earnest by Isabel Myers around World War II. She hoped that through better tools, the horrors of war might be avoided in the future. She also believed that individual happiness could be better achieved if each person could find a more suitable career in a society that values different gifts.

Similarly, while many have explored temperament for over twenty-five centuries, David Keirsey's modernization of the theory was largely motivated by the observation that relationships fail because of the "Pygmalian project"–attempts to mold each other into the image we have for the other person (a mirror image of ourselves), instead of how they are meant to be.

The legacies of these two people ask us to "walk the talk" and "talk the walk"–that is, continually maintain integrity and an unwavering dedication to reality. Theories are useless without people who benefit from and believe in what they mean, and a discussion of character is meaningless without both an ethical compass and

a willingness to acknowledge the fact that people are both similar and different.

For each temperament, there are pitfalls which reflect the Pygmalion Project struggle between self and others. For each temperament there are corresponding gifts and contributions to character.

The Artisan

The Artisan with Others

If their set of relationships, family, organization, or society allows sufficient freedom to act, to make an impact, and to be successful, then Artisans will be more participative and conventional. This is particularly true if the Artisans' impulses and natural talents are culturally popular, such as men in business or sports. However, if they feel constrained, belittled and unable to pursue their interests, they may "drop out," get involved in changing the world, become retaliatory and reckless, or become part of a counter-culture.

Artisan Pitfalls

When an Artisan—or anyone—overidentifies with Artisan values or an Artisan life-theme, or when Artisans are under extreme stress (constraint, boredom, or lack of impact), then they may:

- Hurt themselves or bully others
- Find themselves isolated and limited to a single context or type of environment
- See others as boring, out of touch, or hurtful
- Suddenly find themselves "trying" to have fun somewhere they don't really want to be
- Avoid and disbelieve the atypical, strange, or weird—until it is too late
- Act without thinking
- Believe they are immune to danger and harm
- Avoid introspective self-examination

The Artisan Gift

Artisans have the talent to prize differences as opportunities for success, as the variety and spice of life, with society as an open environment where people can be themselves without infringing on others' freedoms.

The Artisan Contribution to Character

It is our actions, and the attitude that we bring to a situation and people involved, that define who we are. Values, roles, ideas, and personality type are starting points only. Artisan values prompt us to show people who we are through our actions and our attitude!

What Artisan Pitfalls and Gifts have you experienced in yourself and with others.

> *". . . every individual is an exception to the rule."*
> —Carl Jung

The Guardian

The Guardian with Others

If their set of relationships, family, organization, or society is responsible, safe, and secure and provides membership and belonging, then Guardians will be more participative and conventional. However, if they judge that there is a general failure to keep order or fulfill societal contracts, traditions, and obligations, then they will feel pulled between the norms of the larger group and the one branded as "doesn't belong." Guardians usually adopt the lifestyle of the group they identify with, or work to turn back the clock and restore lost values.

Guardian Pitfalls

When Guardians—or anyone—over-rely on Guardian values or a Guardian life-theme, or when Guardians are under extreme stress (abandonment, insubordination or lack of belonging) then they may:

- Place roles above individuals
- Cling to laws or traditions inappropriately in the face of change
- Try to use societal institutions and laws to force other people to accept their help
- Adopt attitudes that go with their group or lifestyle without rigorously examining the real worth of those attitudes
- Suddenly find the world has passed them by
- Blame others for personal failures
- Blame themselves for group failures
- End up settling for a routine that is bad for them

The Guardian Gift

Guardians have the experience to see differences as roles to fulfill and passages of life, as ways to manage, serve, or assist responsibility, with society as a structure that can help people get along with and support each other.

The Guardian Contribution to Character

There is a tendency in all people to confuse feelings or principles about tolerance and compassion with the actual hard work of being compassionate and fulfilling what's needed. Take real responsibility for your behavior for yourself and toward others.

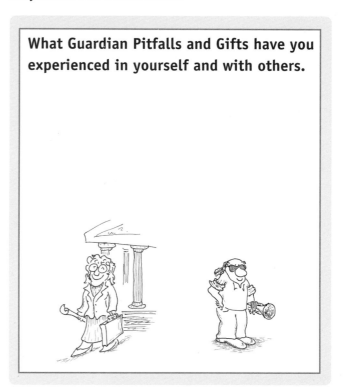

What Guardian Pitfalls and Gifts have you experienced in yourself and with others.

"Conformity is one side of a [person], uniqueness is the other"
—Carl Jung

The Rational

The Rational with Others

If their set of relationships, family, organization, or society is rational and efficient, and allows and supports them to be competent and make progress, then Rationals will be more participative and conventional. However, if their projects, abilities, or vision are blocked for arbitrary reasons, or if they are not allowed control of their own lives and freedom to think for themselves, then they may go it alone, try to change the world, become hard and robotic, or become elitist and arrogant.

Rational Pitfalls

When a Rational—or anyone—overemphasizes Rational values or a Rational life-theme, or when Rationals are under extreme stress (powerlessness, incompetence, lack of knowledge), then they may:

- Try to explain everything from one "truth"
- Push, think of, and treat people as objects
- Explore and plan but not implement because they fear their ideas won't really work
- Cling to principles and projects despite contradictory evidence
- Suddenly find they have lost control or can't focus
- Become revolutionary to overthrow the current system
- End up sacrificing themselves for their projects
- Avoid areas of incompetence

The Rational Gift

Rationals have the ability to understand differences between people as kinds of intelligence, often as specific new abilities or areas to master, with society as a vehicle that can bring progress for all individuals.

The Rational Contribution to Character

All too often, our actions, creations, and beliefs have unintended consequences, and in our attempt to find or hang on to a universal "truth," we may forget truth is an ongoing process of discovery. Rational values remind us to think through the causes and consequences and consider the bigger picture.

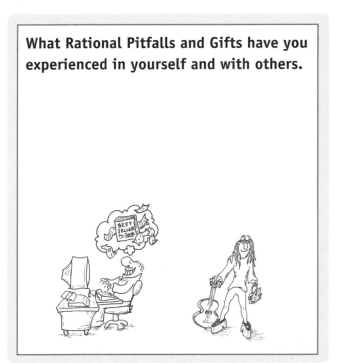

What Rational Pitfalls and Gifts have you experienced in yourself and with others.

The Idealist

The Idealist with Others

If their set of relationships, family, organization, or society is making it possible for the people they value to have a unique identity, meaning, and significance, then Idealists will be more participative and conventional. However, if they perceive valuable people are going unvalued, whether or not they know these people personally, then they may shut out all but the people they like, try to change the world, put on a deceptive mask, or deliberately adopt counter-cultural beliefs.

Idealist Pitfalls

When an Idealist—or anyone—overidealizes Idealist values or an Idealist life-theme, or when Idealists are under extreme stress (insincerity, betrayal, or lack of integrity), then they may:

- Place beliefs above people
- Love the world but find they cannot seem to get along with anyone in it
- Remain honest to themselves but not with others about themselves
- Cling to beliefs in contradiction to reality
- Believe objectivity is impossible
- Suddenly find their perceptions of people are no longer accurate
- Get lost in a relationship or group
- Talk or dream without action

The Idealist Gift

Idealists can possess the wisdom to perceive differences in people as fulfillment of uniqueness, always with more potential to be developed within, with society as a partner that can be in harmony with the individual.

The Idealist Contribution to Character

There is a tendency in human nature to explain our own failings as bad circumstances or "the situation" while explaining others' failures as bad character or "immaturity." Idealist values call us to look inside honestly and be congruent on the outside!

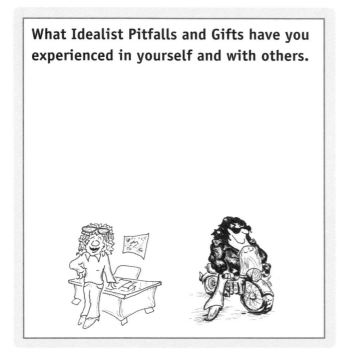

What Idealist Pitfalls and Gifts have you experienced in yourself and with others.

Living Your Moral Vision

It is one thing to be more self-aware, another to grow and change. There are ups and downs, and the moral and ethical quandaries that work and relationship situations reveal to us remind us that we are called to live for both others and ourselves.

Consider how you've chosen to handle—or might handle—temperament specific pitfalls and other difficult situations. Did you:

- Keep quiet or cave in, waiting and seeing, and giving the other person time to re-situate on their own

- Fight back or defend yourself, in the hopes that a little can go a long way, without becoming bogged down

- Step-back or leave, creating more distance or removing yourself completely from the problem situation

- Reason or go "meta", re-examining and opening up to better perceive and better evaluate the situation

These options are interpersonal, not just static internal principles or ideals.

Temperament specific pitfalls and gifts are also interpersonal. Every perception, action, and reaction reflects aspects of others and yourself brought out by the context or relationship, not just you and another person physically together and psychologically separate. Even a "wait and see" reaction is a relationship-driven behavior.

How conscious and changeable is behavior? Behavior happens in patterns. One or more factors lead into or come out of our reactions to a situation; change the stimuli or context and the person may change. Similarly, whether or not we are self-aware, behavior can be altered or shifted. We often repeatedly walk down the same path, seeing the same pitfalls, and stumble time and again. Change may be scary, harmful, premature, or require additional resources such as a model of how to change. But all behaviors serve a purpose. Being conscious includes awareness of a behavior's purpose, and change includes how and when we can change, not just why we should!

- Is the degree of the proposed change appropriate to the needs of the moment, too excessive, or lack relevance? What other kinds of change are possible?

- What specific steps and resources are there to implement a change? There are often more resources than we realize.

- Change occurs in context. We may not feel the need for change because the current situation is adequately comfortable. Consider effects involving others.

- What will tell you change is happening? What are some things, large and small, that may happen if change does or does not occur?

Self-awareness and self-leadership can be empowering, liberating, scary, depressing, joyous, frustrating, or many other emotions—for all involved! Discovering more about who you and who others are may at first feel energizing or it may feel confusing. Similarly, discovering who you are not—or that someone else is simply not a certain way—may strike us as enlightening or it may be depressing. How much can we know about ourselves? Or change about ourselves? Or expect from others? Maintaining a moral center is an ongoing process of re-balancing and change. The next few pages look at paths and patterns to developing all aspects of your type.

"One is always in the dark about one's own personality. One needs others to get to know oneself."
—Carl Jung

Developing All Aspects of Your Type

As we change, we become someone new and unforeseeable.

Your Blueprint Is Inborn

The process of "individuation" calls us to differentiate from the formless potential implied in our blueprint to expression of various processes, parts, and themes; it also calls us to integrate all aspects of our type in a dynamic unified whole. Each flavor of your type represents a facet of your type pattern, and while some flavors may seem alien or very comfortable at present, each facet has an innate inner push to express itself over the course of your life. Look back into the past and forward into your future, and you will find parts of yourself that may strike you as more "immature" or "ideal." On closer inspection, even our ideas about what is mature or ideal shift with each phase of life. In truth, the different flavors of your type are all equally part of who you are—some old, some new, some yet to come. In others of your type, flavors may emerge in a different way or in a different order because of varying circumstances. However, the end result is the same—a spiraling outward and yet inward, continually fulfilling your blueprint, your temperament and type acting as a hidden magnet or gravitational attractor.

For each of us there is a specific inborn blueprint and inner push and pattern for growth over time. By learning the flavors common to each type, we have a map for where we've been and where we can go.

Change is Coded into Your Blueprint

Every day we encounter new avenues for growth and the need to adapt. Also, over a lifetime, any radical changes in personality are clues marking important life milestones. Looking back, your impressions of yourself as a child or teen may initially suggest you were once one flavor, type, or temperament; today, another. Or day to day, you may experience what feels like different facets. This is natural and does not mean you have multiple personality types or have changed type. Rather, change is coded into the genetic blueprint of the self. Behind the scenes there is openness to adaptation, a continual transformational process, and opportunities for metamorphosis. Often this means a temporary shift to a contextual self. Rarely, perhaps two or three times over the course of life, we find that the life-themes and beliefs that have met core needs and values in one environment no longer hold. To cling to an old self will mean an inevitable slide into psychological death. And so, consciously or not, we go inside and reorganize how the core self expresses on the surface. We take a new long-term life-theme or return to an old one in a new way, with new beliefs that better meet our core needs, values, and talents. From this deep transformational process a new flavor emerges. Thus, it is not just that inborn preferences remain constant from one flavor to the next. It is because of adaptation, radical change, and the differences in flavor that we are able to remain true to who we are.

Environment Fulfills Your Blueprint

Although one's temperament and true type are inborn, we take on a great deal of our personality from our parents, siblings, friends, and other role models—consciously or not. It is through the modeling process that the self finds ways to express itself. Sometimes the behaviors taken on are not to our benefit, and our inborn blueprint may not always blossom forth from the soil it is planted in. However, despite outside pressures, the talents, themes and other defining characteristics of our temperament and type have their roots in brain structure and genetics, and the self cannot help but tend to develop in the pattern set down by the blueprint. Environmental effects and the modeling process are not random—we seek needed resources. Given informed choices and congruence with the true self, the behavioral layers that accumulate around our core expand who we are and make it easier to fulfill our innate preferences. Thus, the true self emerges only with the aid of the environment, and the developed self is the search for uniqueness as well as "packaging" and accommodating the demands of family, culture, relationships, and career.

As we change, we are who we've always been only more so.

In living together, social role-taking and feedback from the environment provide models for growth. By learning the flavors of those around us, we have a map of the resources to make growth possible.

Adapting Your Blueprint

Although largely unconscious to start, the developed self can, in part, be consciously influenced through either reorganization or additions. You cannot wholly delete behaviors, but you can redirect and modify them. If, as a child or teen, a life-theme or other overlay is adopted inappropriately as an attempt to fit in, another model may be chosen later. Visiting different places and carefully trying on potential adaptations rounds out who we are, catalyzes creativity, and helps us appreciate the needs and values of all four temperaments. Even seemingly poor choices often come full circle years later to provide unexpected benefits. For example, acting skills learned in the Creative Life-Theme may enrich a foray into the Political Life-Theme later on. Of course, the choices and changes we make must be ecologically sound. That is, each piece must fit with who we are already and with the environment. A poor fit can mean undue conflict and either no real benefit or a loss of energy and time. Working against the natural rhythms of change can be exhausting—those periods of productive transformation punctuated with quieter plateaus. Thus, conscious adaptation is not about hurriedly tacking things on top of who we are or putting on a mask. Half a life may be required to arrive at something energizing and fulfilling. Rather, personal self-leadership is about finding ways to complement one's self in a way that is congruent and harmonious with the natural seasons of life.

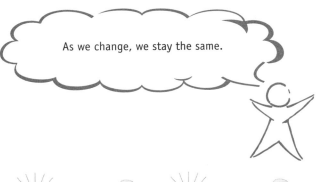

As we change, we stay the same.

John's Journey

Follow John and his lifelong choices and changes. Each step of the way, his INTP themes and Rational core find new expressions.

You can adapt.

John Tries Out an Artisan Life-Theme

Looking back, John sees he was not always so Idealist in flavor. His childhood demeanor was quite different. His first interests pointed to his inborn Rational talents, and beyond that, he told his parents that someday he wanted to design and run his own business. Yet by the time he reached high school, he had already adopted academic and physical interests—good grades and sports—to fit societal and sex-role expectations as well as the "Artisan-Hero" archetype of youth.

John became more participative in his youth, identified with the Rational temperament first and Artisan second, and visited the Academic and Physical Life-Themes, with a vision of entrepreneurial life in his future.

Each of us is called to grow.

John Tries Out an Idealist Life-Theme

John's ENFP father and John's ENFJ business partner for many years were Idealists. They both strongly flavored John's "work persona." His focus in designing workshops and products for people was very much in synch with his INTP talent for design and Rational Life-Theme. But the Idealist skills, mannerisms, and language he has adopted—through the Growth Life-Theme—are catalysts for his global vision of running a business where he can help people help themselves.

John became softer and better adjusted, identified with Rational first and Idealist second, and subsumed his Physical Life-Theme into a larger Growth Life-Theme. Academic and Entrepreneurial Life-Themes have evolved.

We are called to live with others.

John Tries Out a Guardian Life-Theme

Even as John constructed a unique adult self in his thirties, he heard the voice of society to "be establishment" and "be part of the community." Yet not until midlife was he ready to embrace the Community Life-Theme! This previously rejected side became a part of his life when he made himself a part of the lives of his sons. By helping them solve who they were, as opposed to who he was, John ended up incorporating a Guardian Life-Theme first into his personal life and then into his business.

At this point, John has become somewhat more conventional as a parent, identifies with Rational first and Guardian second, and has transformed his academic interests into something more community oriented.

Mastery and understanding are within reach.

John Integrates His Experiences

Only now, a he grows older, does the fruit of John's travels remerge with his core self to produce the kind of mastery and understanding in his profession that, as a Rational, he has worked for since childhood. Now he balances the Community, Growth, and Entrepreneurial Life-Themes and is ready to soon take off with his business side. Ironically, the core self fully lives up to the potential of its innate pattern only at the journey's end. John may soon be ready for a more "local" life of ease and enjoyment.

John's path has given him the opportunity to explore all the flavors of his type as well as visit most of the life-themes and experience and interact with other temperament needs and values besides his own.

Temperament and type are inborn and constant. We "try on" other temperament needs, values, and talents by exploring different life-themes and various flavors of our type.

The Journey Continues

A Framework for Personal Growth

Use the grid below to organize and integrate the different flavors of your type and phases of your life. Think of where you are, where you have been, where you are going, and places you probably cannot visit. You may want to use the four biographical character sketches illustrating your *best-fit type* or refer to the life-themes and examples of those themes in different types, or you may want to think in terms of the different mechanisms that flavor type (global, conventional, participative, etc.)

Remember that some life-themes and flavors may lie in your future! Complete the picture of yourself, using all the pieces you can.

CURRENT EXPRESSION OF SELF

Life-Themes:

Flavors of Type:

PAST EXPRESSION OF SELF

Life-Themes:

Flavors of Type:

FUTURE EXPRESSION OF SELF

Life-Themes:

Flavors of Type:

OTHER EXPRESSION OF SELF (PAST OR FUTURE)

Life-Themes:

Flavors of Type:

As you fill out the timeline above, consider:

1. The core needs and values and the themes of your type pattern

2. Aspects that reflect adaptations and accommodation to the demands of the world

3. Themes and values consistently avoided and ranked last in life

4. Potential themes maybe not in this lifetime, but reflective of a deeper nature and purpose

Locating Yourself on Your Career Map

It's not so much where you're going but how. Some people are "on the fast track"—they are taking an express train to success in life that will bring happiness early and perhaps leave them with significant challenges later on. In contrast, others build toward a goal over their whole lives— a slower pace but often with a big payoff and increasing sense of reward.

Similarly, some people know their aspirations early on; others find themselves contributing to the world and still in search of a specific calling. Having a solid skill set prepares us in either case.

Use the tools below to discover where you are in your career. Consider the quality as well as the quantity of each ingredient and everything that clearly applies. Note what's missing.

The key to career success and happiness lies at the intersection of all four ingredients below.

Where are you now on the road of your life? How far do you have left to go? Are you backtracking or trying different roads? Enjoying the journey itself? Here are important sign posts.

Aspirations - Know the Terrain
When and how did you first know what you wanted to do–in a general way? Specifically? You may have many interests; some have multiple "life missions" while others "have no idea" for many years. Aspirations often seem to be something we just have or don't have. Often, any specific target we pick is simply a first stab at actualizing our aspiration.

- ○ I know my aspirations
- ○ I have chosen a target
- ○ My target and aspirations match

Actualization - Develop a Skill Set
When and how did you experience your first real taste of success and how good did that feel? What baby steps got you to where you could say, "Here I go. This feels right." Some of you may not have reached this point yet. What kind of help - deliberate or serendipitous - was required from others to make this possible? Having the right skills prepares us for opportunities.

- ○ I've taken steps
- ○ I've tasted real success
- ○ There are more steps to take

Commitment - Clarify Your Values
It is one thing to taste success, another to weather problems and digest feedback from others, including the unintended consequences of our good intentions. Big steps may be punctuated by long plateaus or uncertainty. But old skills often can be integrated later in life. The process of internalizing a commitment for ourselves means rechoosing that road again every day.

- ○ I've weathered problems
- ○ I've accepted feedback
- ○ I'm internalizing my commitment

Contributions - Make a Difference
For those of you who've been living in the "prime" of your life, what has success meant? Has it mainly been for yourself and maybe your family or community, or has it been about something much larger and more global in impact that may mean less for those close to you? Real contributions often mean bucking the system in order to make original contributions to your profession.

- ○ I'm making original contributions
- ○ I'm contributing to others
- ○ I'm helping others make contributions

Let's look at John's journey: John, our Idealist-looking Rational, began with a vague high school interest in psychology and pursued that in earnest in his early twenties. For two decades he worked at his education and as a clinical psychologist, as well as heading a family. At age fifty, as his children left home, however, he ended his practice as he knew it and began his own business as a consultant for individuals and teams in businesses and other organizations. He has not only a sense of entrepreneurship but also a sense of mission that evolved slowly but clearly out of his earlier education and work. This choice was hard on his family as well as challenging to him. But weathering ups and downs, John cultivated his expertise as a pioneer and at age seventy found himself suddenly surrounded by devotees and followers of his ideas. Each time he looked back, he saw that the process took much longer than he imagined! Travelling a global, long-range road often does.

Four Steps to Career Success

There are a few universal pieces of advice for everyone, regardless of temperament, type, or flavor.

Choose Your Lifestyle, Then Your Career

Think about what kind of life style you want. Think in specific terms: amount of leisure time, cosmopolitan or country living, and quality family time versus your job. But also think in general terms: an establishment job will not meet someone's counter-cultural attitudes, and a life as an entrepreneur may demand more of a thick skin than someone may be willing to develop. Then consider careers to meet that lifestyle. If you pick career first, based only on existing skills or education, you may likely find yourself unhappy—and lonely—later on. Artisans in particular may find themselves in a career area and then a short way down the road wonder why they feel stuck and aren't enjoying life. The trick is to find an approach that makes it easy to balance both.

| Life Style | ⟶ | Career |

Work from Your Talent, Then Your Challenge Areas

Work from your talent first, then grow outward. Many people have a number of interests–they are talented in one area, currently interested in one or two others that present interesting challenges and opportunities for growth, and they shy away or simply neglect the remainder. When we do what we are talented at, our inborn temperament talents have a way of shining through and attracting success and recognition from others. Our talents may not always interest us at the current time but they will always be there. And when we work from our talents, we can branch out into other areas with a sense of safety, both for ourselves and those who depend on us. Rationals in particular may find themselves exploring numerous challenge areas without taking the time needed to complete expertise in their talent. The trick is to integrate the talent and challenges areas.

| Talent | ⟶ | Challenge Areas |

Do What You Love, Then What Makes Money

Sometimes doing what we love to do does not generate the kind of financial results that we hope for. Other times, caring for others and financial straits can derail our plans. Without money, there are many things you will not be able to do, places you will not be able to go, skills and opportunities you will miss, people you care about that you will not be able to help. But once doors start opening, more doors will open in your path. Do what you love, and then find a way for it to make you money. If you put yourself and who you are into what you are doing, then you will find a challenging but potent reward. And others are attracted to happiness as well as success. Guardians in particular may find themselves making life choices based on money as a form of security instead of finding what they really love. The trick is go more slowly, building patiently from what you enjoy.

| For Love | ⟶ | For Money |

Address Ethics and Integrity, then Self-Interest

It is not enough to simply be happy for oneself. Competition saps vitality, and self-absorption destroys creativity, isolates us, alienates even our true friends, and erodes our spiritual center. Ethics cannot come second. Remember where you came from as well as where you are, and are going. While it may sometimes seem that we have made it on our own, it is the labors and talents of others that have paved the way and support us whether we realize it or not. A life with meaning and integrity, and ethical behavior toward others, is far more than its own reward—it is necessary. Remember your values. Idealists in particular may find themselves in situations where the expectation is self-interest but where ethical questions beg to be addressed. The trick is to work with people who value integrity.

| For Others | ⟶ | For Myself |

Locating Yourself on Your Relationship Map

monality is values, life-theme, career, shared history, type, chemistry, or philosophy of life. As you use the tools below to find where you are on your relationship road map, keep in mind that your honest answers will probably be something both you and the other person can concur on. Consider the quality and quantity of each ingredient. Select everything that clearly applies. Note what's missing.

All interpersonal relationships face similar challenges. It is how you respond that makes or breaks the bond. Relationships should be about two people. There must be a match somewhere–something to relate around–whether the com-

The key to relationship happiness and success lies at the intersection of all four ingredients below.

Where are you in your current relationship? How far do you have left to go? Are you feeling like you are going in circles or playing out the same story and roles? Enjoying yourself? Here are some important signposts.

Chemistry - Be Aware of the Signals

Passion, chemistry, physical appearance–these powerful signals initiate and sustain a couple for the first few years. Biochemistry also bonds mother and child, families and friends. Daily interaction and shared humor, lifestyle, interests, and energy level also help. Passion is a simple immediate force, and little can substitute for physical attraction. Sadly, interest is not always mutual. The paradox is that chemistry is a necessary and yet insufficient ingredient for love. What kind of chemistry do you have?

○ Physical chemistry   ○ Shared interests   ○ Mutual attraction

Compatibility - Go through the Process

Is love supposed to change, complete, or improve us? "Psychological" love–feelings based on deep needs–is a stage to play out and learn from certain roles, stories, and scripts. But it is for learning, not loving. Although psychological compatibility is an important ingredient for love, the desired result is freedom from predefined, unconscious interaction. Love is not about living out a story but creating one together out of shared values. The paradox is to know yourself before love, yet we come to know who we are through knowing others.

○ Complementary values   ○ Compatible life stories   ○ Synergistic effect

Intimacy - Unpack the Meanings

If the other person reports no chemistry or has little interest in compromising, or halting attempts to change you, then you may choose to remain open to different ways of relating and to accept previously hidden aspects of each other, or you may choose to walk away for the time being. The paradox is that only by being apart (whether with longing or alienation) can you begin to understand who the other person is–or, at least, who you really are. Where are you in the relationship tug-of-war?

○ Fostering intimacy   ○ Maintaining autonomy   ○ Open to growth and change

Commitment - Internalize the Relationship

Commitment is an on-going daily willingness to repeatedly meet the other person at his or her view of the world and to respect those perspectives no matter what–you may have checked nothing above and still be committed! We begin to address the paradox of being separate yet together and being together yet separate. Just as uniqueness can be used as a definition of character in the individual, every relationship is called to be different.

○ Maintaining commitment   ○ Contributing to each other   ○ Contributing to others together

---

Let's look at John's relationships: As a Rational, John's strengths are in theorizing and abstract problem solving, and with his background as a psychologist and his Idealist demeanor, he knows quite a bit about and enjoys strategizing relationships! Unfortunately, as the chemistry abated, John discovered that his wife did not appreciate this talent that worked so well with clients and their young children. Something different was needed for the romantic sphere to resolve the subtle tug-of-war. Eventually, he discovered he could redirect his problem-solving talent toward redesigning himself. In the process he began to learn new ways to relate that did not put all the burden for change on him. Now married many years, he and his wife have discovered a whole new way of relating that reaffirms their commitments to each other.

Keys to Relationship Success

Each of us has our own definition of how to relate, and the language of love two people share so easily at some moments can unravel at others. Many times, two otherwise intelligent people believe they are blatantly and obviously communicating their needs and values, when in fact little gets through, because each is working from different core assumptions, interpreting remarks and gestures differently, or looking for an altogether different set of signals. Even seemingly self-explanatory words like passion and trust, intimacy and communication, and commitment and respect can actually hide tremendous differences. Each temperament has its own language.

What you can trust in a relationship is that people will act according to their temperament core needs and values, their type's themes, and the life-themes and attitudes and beliefs that flavor who they are. Even when people agree in principle they go on doing things differently! When there are problems, you do not always need to "fix" them or back off and distance yourself. You can simply give the other person more space to be who he or she is. And you do not need to change each other or yourself, only change what parts of yourselves you show to each other.

Use the guidelines below to help you understand and perhaps discover some strategies for your relationships. These are particularly useful in bringing together the four major ingredients on the previous page.

Idealists

Idealists recognize the importance of sitting with and exploring their values and emotional needs. Insisting they always "be there" for you and not allowing them space to discover other parts of themselves may end your relationship. Idealists also need to allow others more emotional room than they themselves usually need–few people are as talented as Idealists in living with and resolving conflicting feelings. Support Idealists in any new quests or interests with the understanding that they will probably come around again in time to revisit and reintegrate the relationship. They will disassociate from a person they believe can't grow with them. Many Idealists are strong on intimacy and are able to "go there"–and stay there–more than most.

Guardians

Guardians expect a physical space and time set aside—this shows you care and want to include them. This space in your shared lives should be appropriate and long term, not arbitrary, and time spent together should feel comfortable, not rushed or thoughtless. In their desire to monitor and lend a helping hand, Guardians can also leave others without enough privacy, independence, or responsibility for themselves. Reconfirm each other's roles and ask the Guardian to develop a new way to delegate responsibility in the relationship if you want more freedom for yourself. Guardians expectations are often quite traditional. Many Guardians' are strong on commitment and may be ready to commit sooner than others.

RELATIONSHIPS

Rationals

Rationals prefer time to think–a conceptual space to understand what's going on. Ignoring their ideas without listening or attacking reason as a way to understand interpersonal interactions, will leave them cold. Rationals also need to make allowances for others here. Most people do not have the same talent or get the same energizing feeling from analyzing, maximizing and redesigning a relationship. Engage the Rationals' ideas and explicitly ask them to come up with new ones if you disagree. They may not go somewhere in a relationship if they feel incompetent at it and detest when others try to think for them. Many Rationals are strong on compatibility–two people should fit into the big picture of each other's lives with a way to relate.

Artisans

Artisans want space to act, and opportunities for freedom and spontaneity will keep them around. The Artisan who feels trapped or taken advantage of will be resistant and desire escape. Similarly, Artisans can become impatient when others do not act fast enough or act awkwardly, and in their desire to move forward they may end up going their own way or grabbing for themselves the very opportunities the other person needs. Artisans are keenly interested in your motives in a situation, and they want to know what you want in a relationship so they can give that to you. They experience arbitrary rules in relationships as unnecessary obstacles and enjoy surprises. Many Artisans are strong on passion and chemistry.

Rewriting Your Future

Going through the process of writing your own biography is a powerful way to integrate where you are with where you're going.

Before writing a character sketch of yourself, take a moment to reflect on what you've learned about yourself. Consider the three different perspectives below. Begin with the perspective you are most comfortable with.

Incorporate Third Person Perspective

Writing in the third-person voice, looking at yourself from the outside, may feel unsettling at first, but this will allow you to more easily integrate aspects of yourself you may not have considered until now. Briefly describe yourself using your name. (For example, "John is....")

Incorporate First Person Perspective

Writing in the present tense can also be a surprise. We are often told to think of who we are in terms of past experiences. But who we are is something dynamic and alive in the present. By thinking of yourself in the present, you open yourself up to the future. What's going on in your life right now? (Write in the first person: "I am....")

Incorporate Second Person Perspective

How would you feel if you met yourself? What do people say about you and see in you? Think about how different people feel around you. (Write in the second person: "You are....")

Why write from multiple perspectives? Writing about our private self, as well as more public aspects of ourselves, what we do, and who we are helps flesh out our self-image and make it more realistic and reveals commonalties and differences. For example, sometimes looking from a certain perspective will surprise us with new information. Other times we find we have taken information we don't want to look at too much and have hidden that information in one particular perspective. Multiple perspectives allow us to reconcile these surprises, difficulties, and inconsistencies.

Now, as you come home, unpacking your bags after your journey, retrace your steps and finish your map. In addition to considering different perspectives, you may also want to take this time to reflect on what you would like to do with what you have learned so far about yourself–think about the answers you have written down to the questions asked of you earlier. What are your life-themes? Which biographies did you relate to and why? What flavors who you are? Where does this knowledge fit in your life? Incorporate this into your sketch as you write your biography for today. Tomorrow you will be called to write another one.

Write your own character sketch here. If you have trouble, you may want to revisit the character sketches. Use the three guidelines on the facing page and integrate the different voices into a third person narrative, just like the sketches.

▼ C H A R A C T E R ▼

Character is not a separate compartment inside you. It has many meanings. It is an emergent quality that comes out of all that you are and everything you do.

Be Your B.E.S.T.

Build rapport by using what you have learned to create bridges to where others are coming from.

Encourage ethical standards in yourself and others–be open to self-change and novel experiences.

Sustain the process by modeling the positive skills and qualities in others and acting as a model yourself.

Transform your relationships and organization through outcomes that integrate all meanings of character.

Essential Qualities of the Patterns

Temperament

(For a complete explanation of temperament theory, see *Understanding Yourself and Others: An Introduction to Temperament*.)

We have already overviewed temperament. Now let's look at how the temperaments differentiate.

Interaction Styles

Four Patterns to Eight

Each of the four temperament patterns is expressed in either a Directing style or an Informing style.

The Directing interaction style has a time and task focus with a tendency to direct the actions of others in order to accomplish the task in accordance with deadlines, often by either "telling" or "asking." Regarding motivations and process, the Directing style is explicit.

The opposite style is Informing, with a motivation and process focus. Using this style, people tend to give information in order to enroll others into the process. When a task needs to be accomplished, the Informing style engages others, describing outcomes and processes that can be used to complete the task.

Each style has its own best and appropriate use, and most people use both at different times but have more comfort with one. Each temperament pattern is differentiated by a preference for using one of these styles, giving us the eight patterns suggested by the matrix below.

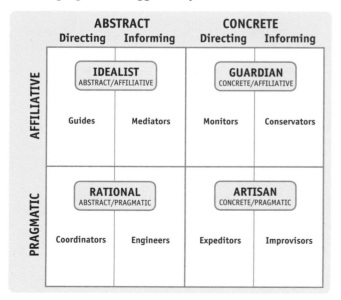

Eight Patterns to Sixteen

Each of these patterns can also be further differentiated by another dimension—a preference for either *Initiating* interactions and a faster pace or for *Responding* to interactions and a slower pace. Now we have sixteen patterns, each with a "theme" as in the matrix below.

Overall, the interaction styles refer to how we typically interact with others. Interaction styles have been described by many in the field of personality and are also frequently described as social styles. The behaviors can be highly situational, but the styles are also inborn patterns that are revealed in the sixteen type patterns.

		ABSTRACT		CONCRETE	
		Directing	Informing	Directing	Informing
AFFILIATIVE	Responding	Chart the Course	Behind the Scenes	Chart the Course	Behind the Scenes
		IDEALIST ABSTRACT/AFFILIATIVE		GUARDIAN CONCRETE/AFFILIATIVE	
	Initiating	In Charge	Get Things Going	In Charge	Get Things Going
PRAGMATIC	Responding	Chart the Course	Behind the Scenes	Chart the Course	Behind the Scenes
		RATIONAL ABSTRACT/PRAGMATIC		ARTISAN CONCRETE/PRAGMATIC	
	Initiating	In Charge	Get Things Going	In Charge	Get Things Going

Carl Jung's Theory of Psychological Type

(For a complete explanation of the cognitive processes, see *Dynamics of Personality Type: Understanding and Applying Jung's Cognitive Processes*.)

In examining individual differences, Swiss psychiatrist Carl Jung differentiated two fundamentally different orientations. He noticed some people seem primarily oriented to the world outside themselves. He called these people *extraverted*. He saw other people as primarily oriented to the world inside themselves. He called these people *introverted*. This extraverted-introverted difference is related to where you focus and recharge your energy. Then Jung noticed that people could be further distinguished by their preferred mental processes. Jung saw two kinds of mental processes used in everyday life—the process of *perception* (becoming aware of) and the process of *judgment* (organizing or deciding).

He then further differentiated two kinds of perception—*Sensation* and *Intuition*. *Sensing* is a process of becoming aware of sensory information. *Intuiting** is a process of becoming aware of abstract pattern information and meanings. Both kinds of information are available to us, but we pay attention to only one kind at a time. Both are necessary and valuable in everyday life.

Likewise, he noted two kinds of judgment—*Thinking* and *Feeling*. Thinking judgments are based on objective criteria and are detached from the personal. Feeling judgments are based on subjective considerations and are attached to personal and universal values. Even the smallest act involves either Thinking or Feeling judgments, and both kinds of decisions are needed and valuable.

Each of these four mental processes can be used in either the external world of *extraversion* or the internal world of *introversion*, producing eight mental processes. Then Jung outlined eight psychological types, each characterized by the predominance of one of these eight mental processes (extraverted Sensing, introverted Sensing, extraverted iNtuiting, introverted iNtuiting, extraverted Thinking, introverted Thinking, extraverted Feeling, and introverted Feeling). In his writings he suggested that each of these eight dominant mental processes was supported by one of two opposing processes and that each of these eight types might vary according to which opposite mental process was used in support of the dominant. For example, the extraverted Sensing type with Thinking would be somewhat different from the extraverted Sensing type with Feeling. Thus, his notions imply sixteen type patterns, each characterized by preferences for the use of two of the eight mental processes.

A Quick Look at the Eight Cognitive Processes

Extraverted Sensing (S_e)

Experiencing, Doing, Observing and Responding, Adapting and Varying, *Present*

> *"This is what is."*
> *"What's next?"*

Introverted Sensing (S_i)

Recalling, Linking, Comparing and Contrasting, Noticing Match and Mismatch, *Past*

> *"This is how it has always been."*
> *"This reminds me of . . ."*

Extraverted iNtuiting (N_e)

Inferring, Hypothesizing, Seeing Potentials, Wondering and Brainstorming, *Emergent*

> *"This is what might be."*
> *"It could be this, or this, or this, or . . ."*

Introverted iNtuiting (N_i)

Foreseeing, Conceptualizing, Understanding Complex Patterns, Synthesizing and Symbolizing, *Future*

> *"This is how it will be."*
> *"Aha, that's it!"*

Extraverted Thinking (T_e)

Being Organized, Coordinating and Sequencing, Segmenting, Checking Against Criteria, *Particular to What Is Here and Now*

> *"This is how to do it."*
> *"People do . . ."*

Introverted Thinking (T_i)

Principles, Categorizing and Classifying, Analyzing, Checking Consistency, *Universal*

> *"This is why . . ."*
> *"It does. . ."*

Extraverted Feeling (F_e)

Being Considerate, Adjusting and Accommodating, Affirming, Checking Appropriateness, *Particular to What Is Here and Now*

> *"This is what we need."*
> *"We do . . ."*

Introverted Feeling (F_i)

Values, Harmonizing and Clarifying, Reconciling, Checking Congruency, *Universal*

> *"This is important."*
> *"I (or you) do . . ."*

The Four Sensing Types

extraverted **Sensing**	with	introverted Thinking	(ESTP)
extraverted **Sensing**	with	introverted Feeling	(ESFP)
introverted **Sensing**	with	extraverted Thinking	(ISTJ)
introverted **Sensing**	with	extraverted Feeling	(ISFJ)

The Four iNtuiting Types

extraverted **iNtuiting**	with	introverted Thinking	(ENTP)
extraverted **iNtuiting**	with	introverted Feeling	(ENFP)
introverted **iNtuiting**	with	extraverted Thinking	(INTJ)
introverted **iNtuiting**	with	extraverted Feeling	(INFJ)

The Four Thinking Types

introverted **Thinking**	with	extraverted Sensing	(ISTP)
introverted **Thinking**	with	extraverted iNtuiting	(INTP)
extraverted **Thinking**	with	introverted Sensing	(ESTJ)
extraverted **Thinking**	with	introverted iNtuiting	(ENTJ)

The Four Feeling Types

introverted **Feeling**	with	extraverted Sensing	(ISFP)
introverted **Feeling**	with	extraverted iNtuiting	(INFP)
extraverted **Feeling**	with	introverted Sensing	(ESFJ)
extraverted **Feeling**	with	introverted iNtuiting	(ENFJ)

---

* We use *Sensing* and *Intuiting* to refer to mental processes rather than *Sensation* and *Intuition* which refer to names of something. Our focus is on the activity, not the "type."

Enter Measurement and the Four Letter Code

When Isabel Myers began developing the Myers-Briggs Type Indicator® (MBTI®), she faced several challenges. One challenge was the beginning of the self-report movement. Prior to that time, psychologists doubted that a self-report format would work. Also, it was a time of "measurement," and the scientific thinking of the time was to understand the world by dividing it into parts. Myers faced the challenge of keeping the holistic quality of Jung's types in the forefront, while meeting the demands of the tests and measurement world. She chose to focus on the opposites in Jung's theory. Jung said that the orientations of extraversion and introversion were dynamically opposite. You can't be in two places at one time! He also said the mental processes were dynamically opposite. Thus, one would have a preference for either Sensing or iNtuiting and Thinking or Feeling in one's day-to-day interactions. The genius of Isabel Myers (and her mother Katharine Briggs) was to develop questions about everyday actions and choices that reflected these underlying opposing preferences.

When the preferences for each of these pairs of opposites were indicated, then the type pattern could be inferred. However, a difficulty remained in how to determine which mental process was dominant in the personality and which was auxiliary. Myers reasoned that we can more readily observe what we do externally, so she decided to add questions to try to find which preferred mental process individuals used in the external world. If they used their preferred judging process to *order* the external world, they would be likely to makes lists and structure their time in advance. If they used their preferred perceiving process to *experience* the external world, they would avoid such planning and structuring and prefer to keep things open-ended. Thus, the *Judging-Perceiving* scale of the MBTI was born. The resultant four-letter code is used around the world to give people insights about themselves.

How Do They Relate?

David Keirsey's temperament patterns (extended out to the four variations of each) meet Jung's theory at the level of the sixteen type patterns. The four-letter code produced by the MBTI stands for one of sixteen type patterns. When it is accurate and verified for the individual, it matches one of Keirsey's sixteen type patterns. While at first glance the matching process looks illogical, it matches at a deep theoretical level when comparing the theoretical underpinnings of each—Jung for the MBTI and Ernst Kretschmer for Keirsey's temperaments. More importantly, it matches on a descriptive, behavioral level.

		ABSTRACT		CONCRETE	
		Directing	Informing	Directing	Informing
AFFILIATIVE	**Initiating Responding**	Foreseer Developer INFJ	Harmonizer Clarifier INFP	Planner Inspector ISTJ	Protector Supporter ISFJ
		IDEALIST ABSTRACT/AFFILIATIVE		**GUARDIAN** CONCRETE/AFFILIATIVE	
		Envisioner Mentor ENFJ	Discoverer Advocate ENFP	Implementor Supervisor ESTJ	Facilitator Caretaker ESFJ
PRAGMATIC	**Initiating Responding**	Conceptualizer Director INTJ	Designer Theorizer INTP	Analyzer Operator ISTP	Composer Producer ISFP
		RATIONAL ABSTRACT/PRAGMATIC		**ARTISAN** CONCRETE/PRAGMATIC	
		Strategist Mobilizer ENTJ	Explorer Inventor ENTP	Promoter Executor ESTP	Motivator Presenter ESFP

Type Dynamics

Type Dynamics is based on the theories of Carl Jung and refers to a hierarchy of cognitive processes (Sensing, iNtuiting, Thinking, Feeling) and a preference for being either in the external world (Extraversion) or the internal world (Introversion). Type dynamics and type development refer to the unfolding of the personality pattern as expressed through the development of the mental processes of perception and judgment. Since the personality is a living system, it is self-organizing—self-maintaining, self-transcending, and self-renewing. Growth and development follow principles of organic development, and there is an order to the evolution of the personality.

The first cognitive process to develop and become more refined is often called the dominant. It is the favorite. The second is often called the auxiliary because it "helps" the first one. It develops second (usually between the ages of twelve to twenty).

Development of the third process usually begins around age twenty and continues until age thirty-five or so. The fourth or least preferred process usually comes into play more between the ages of thirty-five to fifty. These developmental ages are general, not fixed. At these times, we find ourselves drawn to activities that engage and utilize the processes.

Our Shadow Processes, the other four cognitive processes shown in gray, operate more on the boundaries of our awareness. It is as if they are in the shadows and only come forward under certain circumstances.

The following matrix shows the type dynamics patterns represented by the type code. The dominant is listed first, auxiliary second, tertiary third, and least preferred fourth with the shadow processes in gray.

| | ABSTRACT | | CONCRETE | |
	Directing	Informing	Directing	Informing
AFFILIATIVE — Responding	**INFJ** N_i F_e T_i S_e / N_e F_i T_e S_i	**INFP** F_i N_e S_i T_e / F_e N_i S_e T_i	**ISTJ** S_i T_e F_i N_e / S_e T_i F_e N_i	**ISFJ** S_i F_e T_i N_e / S_e F_i T_e N_i
	IDEALIST ABSTRACT/AFFILIATIVE		**GUARDIAN** CONCRETE/AFFILIATIVE	
AFFILIATIVE — Initiating	**ENFJ** F_e N_i S_e T_i / F_i N_e S_i T_e	**ENFP** N_e F_i T_e S_i / N_i F_e T_i S_e	**ESTJ** T_e S_i N_e F_i / T_i S_e N_i F_e	**ESFJ** F_e S_i N_e T_i / F_i S_e N_i T_e
PRAGMATIC — Initiating	**INTJ** N_i T_e F_i S_e / N_e T_i F_e S_i	**INTP** T_i N_e S_i F_e / T_e N_i S_e F_i	**ISTP** T_i S_e N_i F_e / T_e S_i N_e F_i	**ISFP** F_i S_e N_i T_e / F_e S_i N_e T_i
	RATIONAL ABSTRACT/PRAGMATIC		**ARTISAN** CONCRETE/PRAGMATIC	
PRAGMATIC — Responding	**ENTJ** T_e N_i S_e F_i / T_i N_e S_i F_e	**ENTP** N_e T_i F_e S_i / N_i T_e F_i S_e	**ESTP** S_e T_i F_e N_i / S_i T_e F_i N_e	**ESFP** S_e F_i T_e N_i / S_i F_e T_i N_e

Thus we can say that development is dynamic and growing. Development in this sense is like readiness to learn to talk or to walk. We don't have to make children do these, we only need to provide models and opportunities and then stay out of the way. Development can be diverted due to environmental pressures and so is not always in this order as we develop some "proficiencies" using these cognitive processes. Still, the innate preference pattern will remain the same.

Temperament and the MBTI Code

Given the organizing principles of the temperament patterns of needs, values and talents; we like to use the following explanation to link Jung's theory with the four temperaments.

The eight mental processes described by Jung are used to meet the needs and promote the values of the temperament pattern. Certain of these processes suit the pattern so well that the preference for these processes match the preferences indicated by the four letter MBTI codes as follows:

Artisan   _S_P

Artisans can meet their needs for impact and freedom best through the process of extraverted Sensing. This process keeps them tuned in to the needs of the moment and they can readily take tactical actions and seize opportunities. How else would you recognize an opportunity? Thus all Artisans have S and P in their codes. Directing Artisans have S, T, and P in their codes and Informing Artisans have S, F, and P in their codes.

Guardian   _S_J

Guardians can meet their needs for membership and responsibility best through the process of introverted Sensing. They make sure the world will go on by referencing what has gone before. Their vast data bank of stored images and impressions informs the decisions they need to make to preserve the community through logistical actions. All Guardians have S and J in their codes. Directing Guardians have S, T, and J in their codes and Informing Guardians have S, F, and J in their codes.

Rational   _NT_

Rationals meet their needs for knowledge and competence through the mental processes of iNtuiting and Thinking—both in the extraverted and introverted mode. The organizing frameworks and models of the Thinking judgment process used with iNtuiting allow them to readily comprehend complex subjects without experiencing and memorizing which is time consuming. Since they are dealing with the world of theories and strategy, they prefer objective decisions. All Rationals have N and T in their codes. Directing Rationals have N, T, and J in their codes and Informing Rationals have N, T, and P in their codes.

Idealist   _NF_

Idealists meet their needs for meaning and identity through the mental processes of iNtuiting and Feeling—both in the extraverted and introverted mode. Both Feeling judgment processes give them ways to act that are congruent with higher purposes in life (one's own and others'). It is only through examination of the meaning and the pattern information provided by the iNtuiting process that they can apprehend what will be or what is significant in the long run. All Idealists have N and F in their codes. Directing Idealists have N, F, and J in their codes and Informing Idealists have N, F, and P in their codes.

Questions and Answers

Where do the biographies come from? Have they been tested with people?

At least eight people of each of the sixteen types—at least thirty-two people of each temperament—were interviewed or studied in order to create the biographies. After expert feedback, several in-depth studies with college students guided the editing process.

If I find a character like me, then is that my temperament and type? And if not, who am I?

The character sketches may feel ideal for helping people improve their understanding of themselves, particularly for the "hard" cases. Keep in mind, however, that these sketches will not work for everyone and may be very misleading in some cases.

I noticed the MBTI four-letter codes. Do the sketches represent different "subtypes"?

Each of the four biographies represents a different aspect of each of the sixteen type themes that instruments like the MBTI attempt to detect. There are many more characters that could have been written, but space and memory suggested a limit of four - a balance between simplicity and diversity. In fact, most people like two or three of the biographies, not just one. All versions of our type exist within us, with some sides (characters) showing themselves more then others.

These people are very successful and feel somewhat hard to live up to. Can this be me?

The biographies are written from the third person point of view, with an emphasis on portraying people who are highly successful in what they do and who they are - almost heroic in nature. Some people do find the biographies, as examples of character, "hard to live up to." The characters suggest our potential, representing an "ideal self" or dreams and aspirations.

Does gender matter? Some characters are men and others are women.

The sex of the characters is arbitrary. Both genders are represented equally to help people feel comfortable. Keep in mind, however, that the author is male, which influences the tone of how the characters are presented. Inevitably, these are people as seen through the eyes of the author.

I see that some characters are meant to be like me, but they don't feel quite right.

Because the biographies tend to be more career and task focused, as opposed to relationship and past-experiences focused, some people may feel the tone of the biographies is not quite right for them. You are encouraged to write your own biography to explore this other side.

What about ethnic background, social class, and other factors?

An attempt was made to incorporate multicultural observations that have been made by people in the psychological type community. Most notably, your preferences may be significantly different from your society's modal type, which can be both a blessing and a curse!

How else can I use the biographies to help with my relationships?

Many people are used to dissecting relationship issues or implementing a laundry list of techniques to save their relationships. But just as we are not made up simple parts, neither are other people. To get the most out of this, follow pages 68 and 69 to write a biography of the other person you have in mind, in their voice, with their needs and values, idiosyncrasies and flavoring. The process may even give you answers to questions you haven't asked yet!

Are the life-themes related to other models?

Although the life-themes were largely developed from empirical observations, they seem to represent modern day equivalents of how we express classical human archetypes. For example, the Physical Life-Theme often expresses the Warrior archetype, the Academic Life-Theme, the Magician, and so on. The life-themes also appear to roughly correspond to one perspective of the chakras in Eastern teachings.

How can I use the biographies with other facilitative tools?

Psychological instruments, interest inventories and similar paper-and-pencil assessment tools are data points only. A tremendous effort was made to find a *best-fit type* during the informal studies using the biographies and through the use of multiple methods and models—from the MBTI to temperament theory. Unlike many "parts" or "trait" approaches, however, the biographies represent a holistic look at career, values, personality themes, and relationships. Character emerges from the interaction of these themes.

YOUR FEEDBACK

We would appreciate any feedback you can give us to improve this product. Please visit our Web site
www.telospublications.com/feedback

For the Facilitator

For the Type Knowledgeable

While the self-discovery process incorporated in this book can stand alone, it can be a useful adjunct to other books in the Understanding Yourself and Others™ series, as well as the MBTI®, Strong Interest Inventory®, and similar instruments that are compatible with temperament and type theory. Here are some examples.

Working with Multiple Models

The three INTPs below all clearly demonstrate the theme of the INTP - engineering and design - as well as the Rational temperament needs and values of knowledge, mastery and competence. At the same time, each one has a very different look and feel. Each one is a different "flavor" of INTP.

Mark has worked for many years as an engineer for a large traditional company. He scored ISTJ on the MBTI at work but self-identified with INTP once he separated out his "work self" from his "core self." Although his interest in and approach to design are classic INTP themes, his suit-and-tie appearance, sports hobbies and conservative background give him a more Guardian look and feel. He also fell into the Investigative theme on the SII, and his responses to some of the STEPII subscales helped him explain what, specifically, his job was asking of him as well as other specific ways to meet his needs.

Rational INTP - Establishment (Guardian) Life-Theme

Linda is a psychologist and looks more Idealist to many people. She scored INFP on the MBTI, and with STEPII subscales as participative and initiating, she continues to explore a preference for extraversion. To no one's surprise, she spends a lot of time facilitating small groups. However, her main interest is designing training programs. The INTP design theme clearly matched for her when she saw that her SII interest in the social theme was actually highly theoretical in nature, and none of the INFP biographies really appealed to her.

Rational INTP - Growth (Idealist) Life-Theme

Tim is an artist and musician. He works with music on a computer, and he travels quite a bit with his band, deliberately avoiding an "establishment" life. Tim is not interested in conventional instruments like the MBTI, although he read the theory on his own and had many probing questions. He found the STEPII scales an interesting way to define himself in more detail and quickly connected this to his personal "flavor." It also explained for him why his approach to music was so theoretical and not as "feeling" as another band member's. Many people mistake Tim for an Artisan, and the facilitator suggested he read the ISTP biographies as a check against INTP, but ISTP struck him as too concrete and directive.

Rational INTP - Creative (Artisan) Life-Theme

Important Reminders to Clients

Clients with previous type knowledge or another theoretical background may find they need to "unlearn" some ideas, while those new to type may require reinforcement in some areas:

1. People of the same type, in the same situation, may make very different choices–*which* choices comes with maturity, but *how* we make choices fits with temperament and type.
2. The life-themes are not skills, temperament intelligences, or talents. They are worlds that encourage particular attitudes and beliefs about our values. They are "metavalues."
3. Anyone of any type can be "a born natural" in sports or possess artistic or musical talent or be a leader. What defines us is how we combine and bring to fruition our skills.
4. Temperament and type by themselves do not reveal the total scope of human nature, and even understanding and applying the theory takes longer than one might think. Type is a "language" or "lens."
5. Self-discovery is a process. It is just as important to reject what doesn't fit as to incorporate what does and to remain open to something that may fit better.

Honing Your Expertise

This book is also meant for the type-knowledgeable practitioner. When asked, experts say "type takes many years," and cross-discipline studies suggest what leads to expertise:

- Thorough understanding of multiple theories and how they interrelate, and being able to apply the theory "cold." Simple either/or rules are only an early part of the learning process.
- Extensive experience with many, many different people, providing specific examples and experiences to draw upon. Stereotypes are only a way to begin.

There is a saying about the sixteen types: "Every ENFP is like every other ENFP, is like some other ENFP, is like no other ENFP."

The biographies can, by themselves, act as a catalyst to your learning process by providing specific examples - some of which might require years to encounter in daily life.

Foundations of Temperament

Kretschmer, Ernst. *Physique and Character*. London: Harcourt Brace, 1925.

Roback, A. A. *The Psychology of Character*. New York: Arno Press, [1927] 1973.

Spränger, E. *Types of Men*. New York: Johnson Reprint Company, [1928] 1966.

More about Temperament

* Berens, Linda V. *Understanding Yourself and Others: An Introduction to Temperament*. Huntington Beach, Calif.: Telos Publications, 1998.

Choiniere, Ray, and David Keirsey. *Presidential Temperament*. Del Mar, Calif.: Prometheus Nemesis Books, 1992.

Delunas, Eve. *Survival Games Personalities Play*. Carmel, Calif.: SunInk Publications., 1992.

Keirsey, David. *Portraits of Temperament*. Del Mar, Calif.: Prometheus Nemesis Books, 1987.

Keirsey, David, and Marilyn Bates. *Please Understand Me*. 3d edition. Del Mar, Calif.: Prometheus Nemesis Books, 1978.

* Keirsey, David. *Please Understand Me II*. Del Mar, Calif.: Prometheus Nemesis Books, 1998.

The Sixteen Personality Types

* Baron, Renee. *What Type Am I?* New York: Penguin Putnam, 1998.

* Berens, Linda V., and Dario Nardi. *The 16 Personality Types: Descriptions for Self-Discovery*. Huntington Beach, Calif.: Telos Publications, 1999.

Berens, Linda V., and Olaf Isachsen. *A Quick Guide to Working Together with the Sixteen Types*. Huntington Beach, Calif.: Telos Publications, 1992.

Brownsword, Alan W. *It Takes All Types!*. Nicasio, Calif.: HRM Press, 1987.

* Fairhurst, Alice M., and Lisa L. Fairhurst. *Effective Teaching, Effective Learning*. Palo Alto, Calif.: Consulting Psychologists Press, Inc., 1995.

* Isachsen, Olaf, and Linda V. Berens. *Working Together: A Personality Centered Approach to Management*. 3d edition. San Juan Capistrano, Calif.: Institute for Management Development, 1991.

* Tieger, Paul D., and Barbara Barron-Tieger. *Do What You Are*. Boston, Mass.: Little, Brown and Company, 1995.

* Tieger, Paul D., and Barbara Barron-Tieger. *Nurture by Nature*. Boston, Mass.: Little, Brown and Company, 1997.

Jung/Myers Model

* Berens, Linda V. *Dynamics of Personality Type: Understanding and Applying Jung's Cognitive Processes*. Huntington Beach, Calif.: Telos Publications, 1999.

Brownsword, Alan W. *Psychological Type: An Introduction*. Nicasio, Calif.: HRM Press, 1989.

Harris, Anne Singer. *Living with Paradox*. Pacific Grove, Calif.: Brooks/Cole Publishing, 1996.

Jung, Carl G. *Psychological Types*. Princeton, N.J.: Princeton University Press, 1971.

Myers, Katharine and Linda Kirby. *Introduction to Type: Dynamics and Development*. Palo Alto, Calif.: Consulting Psychologists Press, 1995.

Myers, Isabel Briggs; Mary H. McCaulley and Naomi L. Quenk. *MBTI Manual: A Guide to the Development and Use of the Myers-Briggs Type Indicator*. Palo Alto, Calif.: Consulting Psychologists Press, 1998.

Sharp, Daryl. *Personality Type, Jung's Model of Typology*. Toronto, Canada: Inner City Books, 1987.

Quenk, Naomi. *In the Grip*. Palo Alto, Calif.: Consulting Psychologists Press, 1985.

Systems Thinking

Bateson, Gregory. *Mind and Nature: A Necessary Unity*. New York: Bantam Books, 1979.

Bateson, Gregory. *Steps to an Ecology of Mind*. New York: Ballantine Books, 1972.

Capra, Fritjof. *The Web of Life*. New York: Anchor Books, Doubleday, 1996.

Oshry, Barry. *Seeing Systems: Unlocking the Mysteries of Organizational Life*. San Francisco, Calif.: Berrett-Koehler Publishers, 1996.

Wheatley, Margaret J. *Leadership and the New Science*. San Francisco, Calif.: Berrett-Koehler Publishers, 1992.

Wheatley, Margaret J., and Myron Kellner-Rogers. *A Simpler Way*. San Francisco, Calif.: Berrett-Koehler Publishers, 1996.

Biological Basis of Behavior

Ornstein, Robert. *The Roots of the Self: Unraveling the Mystery of Who We Are*. San Francisco: HarperCollins, 1993.

Hamer, Dean, and Peter Copeland. *Living with Our Genes: Why They Matter More Than You Think*. New York: Bantam Doubleday Dell, 1998.

Colt, George Howe. "Life Special: Were You Born That Way?" *Life* (April 1998): 38–50.

Cultural Influences

Hofstede, Geert. *Culture and Organizations: Software of the Mind*. New York: McGraw-Hill, 1997.

Hypnosis, NLP and Ericksonian Methods

O'Connor, J., and J. Seymour. *Introducing NLP: Neuro-Linguistic Programming*. San Francisco, Calif.: The Acquarian Press, 1993.

Bandler, R., and J. Grinder. *The Structure of Magic, Volume 1: A Book about Language and Therapy*. Palo Alto, Calif.: Science and Behavior Books, 1975.

Bandler, R., and J. Grinder. *The Structure of Magic, Volume 2: A Book about Communication and Change*. Palo Alto, Calif.: Science and Behavior Books, 1980.

MacDonald, W., and R. Bandler. *An Insiders Guide to Sub Modalities*. Cupertino, Calif.: Meta Publications, 1989.

James, T., and W. Woodsmall. *Time Line Therapy and the Basis of Personality*. Cupertino, Calif.: Meta Publications, 1988.

Applying Multiple Models

Nardi, D., and L. Berens. "Wizards in the Wilderness and the Search for True Type." *Bulletin of Psychological Type* 21, no. 1 (1998). (This article is available on the Temperament Research Institute Web site—www.tri-network.com/articles)

On the Internet

Temperament Research Institute, www.tri-network.com

*Recommended for Beginners

Many of these products are available on the Temperament Research Institute website—**www.tri-network.com/catalog**